Norfolk Cottage

Ion Trewin

Michael Joseph – London

First published in Great Britain by Michael Joseph Ltd
52 Bedford Square, London WC1B 3EF

© 1977 by Ion Trewin

ISBN 0 7181 1595 3

Film set in Great Britain by DP Media, Hitchin
Printed by Hollen Street Press at Slough
and bound by Dorstel Press, Harlow

For Sue
together we did it

and

to the memory of Isla Merry

Contents

MAINLY PLAY

POSTSCRIPT

Introduction

I first wrote about Bank Cottage in *The Times* in May 1975, more than a month before the builders moved out. Immediately letters reached me from readers, the telephone in my office rang incessantly with requests for more information about the particular scraping tool I recommended, or the paint pads, or the spiral screwdriver. As more articles appeared so the calls and the letters increased. I found myself discussing cottages, not literary gossip at publishers' parties.

Bank Cottage is our pleasure. It began as a cold-blooded investment; it has become an alternative way of life, a release from the tensions of the capital, an introduction to the delights of the country for two children, city-born and brought up. I was surprised therefore at the minority who objected to the whole idea of my second home. To a few it is, I am sure, nothing more than jealousy, but to the others there is a political point that they feel must be made. To one such complainant I remonstrated: if we hadn't restored Bank Cottage, perhaps it would have fallen down as no one else seemed keen to take the plunge. The response from the other side was vulgar in the extreme, followed by the receiver being slammed down.

In fact it would be wrong to imply that only townees restore country property. The three one-up and one-down cottages next to ours have been bought by a local businessman for conversion into a single home for himself and his wife. But they are the exception: generally speaking, Norfolk families who were brought up in damp, insanitary terraced cottages yearn for the modern bungalows and semi-detached houses on the new estates.

In my articles in *The Times* I included much practical lore as I had gained, coupled with notes on new products and useful gadgets. This is, however, not a do-it-yourself handbook, but an account of an adventure: in finding, purchasing, restoring and now enjoying a cottage in a most congenial village by a river in Norfolk.

What we have achieved could never have been done alone so let me thank here all those who have helped Sue and me, especially Antony Askew, friend and mentor; Donald Noyce, architect; Ray Noyce, builder; Mr Hurst, lately of the Public Health Department, Downham Rural District Council; Sally and Bob Edwards, neighbours; and the Reverend Cyril Rogers, lately Vicar of St Germans. As for the book, my gratitude to John Johnson and Alan Brooke for encouraging me to write it, and Antony Askew again, for his generosity in putting his photographic records at my disposal.

Finally let me say that this is a very personal book. My experiences are reported as I saw them, likewise life in our village. I wondered at first if we would be accepted, but it is one of the many reasons for saying regularly 'praise be for our Norfolk cottage!' that we aren't treated as interfering strangers from London.

Wiggenhall St Germans and Highgate, July 1976

Mainly Work

CHAPTER ONE

In which

Bank Cottage is viewed for the first time, the
Public Health Inspector's man gives his verdict
and we learn the pitfalls
of chasing a mortgage

The road to our village from King's Lynn makes six right-angle bends in four miles. The first time I did the journey, in the estate agent's car, the sun was thawing the roads, still treacherous with black ice, each bend a slow-motion skid that took my mind off the landscape of 'wheat, beet and 'taters' (a phrase that we were to pick up from our vicar two summers later). Not that in April one could see much more than a green stubbling of the rich, silt soil as the first shoots braved the late spring, but the buds were swelling on the apple orchards that also dominate this part of north-west Norfolk. In London the first blossom was already brightening sheltered garden corners, but East Anglia seemed weeks behind.

It was the Thursday before Easter 1973, a crisp, cloudless morning, made brighter for me by the prospect of a pantiled, burnt brown brick Norfolk cottage. I had spied it in the window of a King's Lynn estate agent, a colour photograph that, in retrospect, was skilfully angled to include what appeared to be some sort of summer-house at the bottom of the garden. The cottage seemed on the edge of a grassy bank; it had a knee-high white paling fence at the front and side, even a television aerial sprouting from the chimney, but the caption to the photograph named only the village – St Germans – and the price: £6,000.

I was unused to an estate agent's company. In the eight months we had been house-hunting in Norfolk normal practice was to collect keys, plot a course and fend for oneself, the particular cottage we were intent on looking at usually being unoccupied, if not derelict. But on this occasion, the girl in the estate agent's office explained that as this cottage was still furnished, the keys were in possession of a relation, and I would need to be accompanied.

The agent looked as prosperous as only a housing boom could endow. Gazumping was a current vogue word and occurrence. We talked – between the skids – of the attractions of this part of Norfolk. Prices had been soaring for twelve months and more. What a pity it was that I hadn't thought of looking for a cottage a year before when prices were half what they were now. St Germans – or Wiggenhall St Germans, to give its full name – was signalled by a large, carved illustrated sign in relief. Our mutual enthusiasm was dampened a moment later when the agent found that the relation holding the key

had gone Easter shopping in Lynn. It was annoying, but we perked up at the thought that old cottages are rarely burglar-proof. We drove two hundred yards farther into the village, parked on an expanse of gravel outside the appropriately named Central Stores (it being opposite church, pub and garage) and walked up an unprepossessing cul-de-sac. There at the end on the right, nestling closer into the bank than I had expected from the picture, was the property I had come to inspect, simply called on the estate agent's prospectus – 'The Cottage, the Riverbank'.

River? I hadn't realised the proximity to water. Hauling myself up the steep and grassy slope (daffodils, crocuses and primroses would look good here, I thought immediately) I paused for a moment to look down on to the Great Ouse, swiftly flowing, muddy and surprisingly wide. For a moment, the cottage was forgotten: as if on cue two gulls circled angrily and touched down into the water. The agent, meanwhile, was trying to break into the cottage, but with no success. He even enlisted the aid of a builder working on a cottage on the other side of the cul-de-sac – a cottage, incidentally, where modernization was almost complete – but the window catches were rusted solid and it wouldn't have done to shoulder down the front door.

I had come to King's Lynn, not with this cottage in mind, but for an auction the previous evening for a later Victorian detached house at Dersingham, a village to the north of the Sandringham royal estate. The vendors had obviously chosen the right moment to sell: at the auction – in a King's Lynn pub – bidding was brisk, rocketing through the reserve to settle at £8,450 – or far above what we could afford. Sue and I had been looking for something cheaper and mortgageable, a cottage for holidays and weekends, a retreat from our north London flat. We felt the need to own property before prices rose completely beyond our reach. We chose Norfolk, because much of the country is accessible in two to three hours from north London, yet with no more than forty-five minutes additional drive (at the maximum) we could be at the coast. But what clinched it, I think, was that prices were still comparatively reasonable, at least by London standards.

Our ideal was something with three bedrooms, not too large a garden (we were, after all, going to be absent for long stretches), in a village and reasonably near a railway station (we already envisaged that I would commute Fridays and Mondays when Sue and the children were there during the holidays). In haphazard fashion we scoured Norfolk from its far north-east, working steadily west and for one brief week the previous Christmas at Foulsham, a pretty village to the north-west of Norwich (and not far from Parson Woodforde's celebrated parish of Weston Longeville *) we thought we had found our ideal, a cottage on the market for only £2,900. We must have appeared too eager as the vendor promptly withdrew it when we made a firm offer. Seven months later it was sold at auction for over £6,000. Perhaps it was just as well. With only a yard at the back – reached via a covered passage – it fronted directly onto the village main street. No place, in fact, for London children wanting freedom of the countryside.

My road atlas is ringed with the villages we investigated: I remember an interesting terrace of cottages, one with a well, on a hillside at the delightfully named Burgh-next-Aylsham (in itself an attractive market town), but remember nothing of the property in Blofield, Lenwade or Worstead. Surely it was the cottage at Briston that smelled of drains? The small town of Holt I recall more for The Feathers, its comfy old coaching hotel. I longed to live in Little Snoring – or was it neighbouring Great Snoring? – if only for the name. The Walsingham estate appeared to have a dozen empty cottages in nearby villages. We put a note through the agent's door, while the children played with the pump in the square, but only one came on the market, and then by the rare procedure of tender. It was the nastiest cottage of them all, so we didn't follow it up. I liked Fakenham as a market town, but the cottage at the intriguingly-named Whissonsett was about to be overshadowed by new housing (and when we passed by three years later, after a day at Fakenham races, the cottage had been pulled down). Brisley and Weasenham All Saints have blurred in my memory as have Litcham and Great Massingham. Swaffham, which once boasted three different railway routes from London, seemed too far from the coast.

* *The Diary of a Country Parson 1758-1802*, by James Woodforde. London, Oxford University Press, 1935.

ESTABLISHED 1768

CRUSO & WILKIN
INCORPORATING INGRAM WATSON & SON

HORACE O. WILKIN
M.B.E., F.R.I.C.S. F.I.Arb.
THOMAS M. WILKIN
F.R.I.C.S.
GEORGE A. TURNER
F.R.I.C.S.
BERNARD C. MATTHEWS
A.R.I.C.S.
CONSULTANT
ROBERT T. HAY
E.R.D. F.R.I.C.S. F.S.V.A. A.M.T.P.I.

CHARTERED SURVEYORS
CHARTERED AUCTIONEERS AND ESTATE AGENTS

KING'S LYNN
HUNSTANTON
AND FAKENHAM

TELEPHONE:
KING'S LYNN 3111 (4 LINES)
STD 0553 3111

27 TUESDAY MARKET PLACE
KING'S LYNN

All properties are offered subject to Contract and remaining unsold

Norfolk

Wiggenhall St. Germans   King's Lynn

A BRICK AND FLINT COTTAGE OF CHARACTER

occupying a delightful riverside position in the popular village of St.
Germans
close to local shops and post office
and only 4 miles from the expanding town of King's Lynn

(close to bus route)

THE COTTAGE

THE RIVER BANK

£5,500
PRICE   £6,000   FREEHOLD

Vacant possession upon completion.

Sitting Room.   Kitchen/Diner.   Two Bedrooms.   Stores.
Outside W.C.   Main Water and Electricity.

Requiring modernisation and conversion: grants probably
available.

B

17

We were beginning to know our way around the estate agents' blurbs. 'St Germans – £6,000' was described thus:

A brick and flint cottage of character
occupying a delightful riverside position in popular village
close to local shops and post office
and only four miles from the expanding town of King's Lynn
(close to bus route)
Price £6,000 Freehold
Vacant possession upon completion
Sitting room/Kitchen-Diner/Two bedrooms/Stores/Outside WC
Mains water and electricity
Requiring modernization and conversion: grants probably available

I was under no illusion at the meaning of the words 'of character' and 'requiring modernization'. But I liked what I saw. I don't remember being extravagantly enthusiastic; certainly no flash of precognition told me that here was the cottage we had spent nine months searching for. Rather it was the location that first captured my heart: a river by one's door. The idea grew in my mind. Memories from childhood of Arthur Ransome and Kenneth Grahame flooded back. In our case the Great Ouse was only twenty feet from our cottage, it was tidal, too, which meant that the sea really was within easy reach. I returned to London most enthusiastic, although worried that Sue might rule it out because the river would be thought too risky for two children, Simon, then aged six, and Maria, two. But Sue seemed unconcerned – perhaps, in retrospect, she sensed in my enthusiasm that here indeed was something special. Thus on Easter Sunday she travelled by train to King's Lynn (the journey from London takes just a shade over two hours) and then sampled the local taxi service for that final four miles to the cottage.

'I remember' [says Sue] 'locating the keyholder via her back door and the smell of lunch cooking. She was obviously about to begin eating, but she wouldn't give me the key which I said I would return later. I was told that the property was still furnished with valuable furniture, therefore I couldn't possibly be allowed in alone. Therefore,

18

I took the lady in my waiting taxi, assuming it was some way away, but in no time at all we were there. The door was unlocked and what a surprise – a beautiful pianola propped up against the parlour wall. I thought, so this was the valuable property, which indeed it was. Unfortunately it was to be removed. Otherwise I remember the cooker, which seemed in remarkably good condition, and odd bits and pieces.

'It was the position that attracted me. The house itself, well, I realized an awful lot would have to be done to make it habitable. But I liked the river. It was the best situation we had seen, and I knew why it had attracted Ion.

19

'Sadly I couldn't stay long. The lady with the key had her lunch to return to, and the taximan was waiting to take me back to Lynn.'

It was at this point that I began to keep a diary:

April 23 (Easter Monday): We talked about nothing but the cottage most of today. After nine months of hopes and disappointments we are cautiously optimistic. It is agreed that I shall enquire about the possibilities of a mortgage from a friendly broker tomorrow.

April 24: The broker sets mortgage hopes in train with Abbey National Building Society. Estate agent, when phoned to confirm our interest, reveals that 'closure order' exists on the property. Ignorance is bliss, but he suggests that if we wish to know more we should speak to the public health inspector at the local council offices. If we really are still interested, says the agent, guardedly I feel, perhaps we would like to approach a local specialist firm in damp proofing for a free estimate. I do.

April 25: Mr Hurst, of public health inspector's office of the Downham Rural District Council, is most helpful. 'I don't like talking about these things on the phone', he says. 'I'd much prefer to show you what's wrong and what needs doing.' He agrees to meet me off the London train tomorrow.

April 26: I take the 8.36 a.m. from Liverpool Street and sure enough two hours later Mr Hurst is at Downham station to meet me. If this is what is meant by Norfolk courtesy then we couldn't have chosen a better county. During the fifteen-minute drive to St Germans we talk about many things, but principally the matter in hand, and most particularly the Government's improvement grants. He's firmly in favour because several hundred properties have been improved with their help in the Downham area. The key to the cottage is still with the relation, but most of the furniture has now been removed and only the pianola is left. Mr Hurst is a cheery soul, even with grim news to relate. As we move from room to room he emphasizes the faults that will have to be rectified: the front doorway and downstairs ceilings are too low; the floors and walls are riddled with damp; neither of the cottage's *two*

20

staircases meets modern safety standards; the roof, although better than many, will have to be stripped, felted and retiled; the electrical wiring will have to be renewed. But there are compensations, and I see that Mr Hurst shares my enthusiasm for having a river at our door. But first we must be practical: a kitchen and bathroom could be accomodated in the lean-to brick outhouse at the back. Upstairs, by the less rickety of the staircases, and Mr Hurst asks if I would have any objection to making a sitting-room out of one of the first-floor rooms ('that way you'll get a magnificent view westwards across the Ouse'). By his reckoning complete renovation and modernization would cost about £3,500 – with about £1,000 of this being accounted for by grants. Over a lunchtime drink he produces a list of architects and with a little prompting marks three who might be interested in drawing up plans.

May 2: The broker phones to say he needs a cheque for Abbey National's survey fee. 'It should take ten days to a fortnight. Don't be impatient,' he says.

May 3: Phone estate agents to say that Abbey National are taking a look. But the agent is not too hopeful. 'It is an old property, you see.'

May 17: The post brings our first set-back. The Abbey National refuses us a mortgage: ' . . . does not afford a suitable security for an advance from the Society's funds . . . needs a considerable amount spent on it'. Damn! I phone the Abbey National's man and discover, on an off-the-record basis, that the valuation report from their surveyor (in fact another King's Lynn estate agent) reckons that the property is sound basically and the village up-and-coming. In fact he wouldn't deter us from trying to find alternative finance – why not approach the local council? I telephone the estate agent (tail very much between my legs) and pass on the bad news. He is sorry, but not dismayed. 'The council here in King's Lynn sometimes gives mortgages on old property, even if they're not in the borough.' He agrees to have the appropriate forms forwarded.

May 19: Forms arrive. Estate agent asks me to phone him first to discuss application, pointing out that we'll have to overcome the hurdle of not actually living in the area. 'For heaven's sake', he insists, 'don't say you want it as a holiday cottage.'

May 20: I send off mortgage application to the Borough of King's Lynn.

May 25: King's Lynn acknowledges application and asks me to telephone. As expected the council is concerned that it might just be a second home. I counter that we don't actually possess any other property, our London flat being rented and in a house owned by Sue's mother. I add that it is our intention to make the cottage our home, even if we have to spend much of our working life in London. This seems to satisfy the council's man.

June 2: Letter from council. Our mortgage application has been approved, or, in official language: the Council is prepared, subject to satisfactory title, to make the following offer –

Advance	Repayment period	Current interest rate	Monthly repayment
£4,400	20 years	8½% variable	£38.45

Underneath is typed, against a red asterisk, 'the loan is subject to the conditions listed on the attached sheet' – and there follow eight paragraphs devoted to specific modernizations and repairs. I work out that the £4,400 advance is, in fact, an eighty per cent mortgage, assuming that the council value the property at £5,500. Thus we decide that we should offer £5,500 rather than the asking price of £6,000. The estate agent gives nothing away but says he will pass on offer to vendors. Cross fingers and wait.

June 11: Estate agent phones me at *The Times*: our offer is accepted. I phone Sue's family solicitor and ask him to take charge of the legal side.

June 13: Richard, our solicitor, writes: 'I received details from estate agent with a copy of their Sale Particulars. The cottage looks quite

22

charming from the photograph which does not show any of the defects at all.' Who said that the camera never lies?

June 23: Richard writes to say draft contract received: he is puzzled by a reference to a cesspool which is apparently shared with the cottage next door. He is asking Downham Rural Council if the eight paragraphs of specific modernizations and repairs stipulated by the neighbouring Borough of King's Lynn, will also be sufficient to have closure order lifted.

June 25: I reply saying that I had been told that mains drainage is being laid in the village, so does cesspool really matter?

June 28: Richard writes (our letters crossed) to say that he has discovered that our cottage and the one next door used to have the same owner.

July 11: Richard suggests that the mains drainage I am so enthusiastic about will probably be connected only to the nearest main road and that we will have to pay for connection jointly with other people in the terrace. He also sends us the contract to sign. This we have to return with cheque in favour of vendors' solicitors for £550, which is ten per cent deposit required on exchange of contracts.

July 13: (my birthday): We sign contract, send cheque.

July 16: Contracts about to be exchanged says Richard, who adds: 'You are binding yourselves to buy the property at a future date . . . probably not more than one month after the date of the contract.'

July 29: We go off on holiday to North Cornwall, to tumbledown, but delightful cottage in tiny village near Wadebridge.

August 9: Richard writes to say that everything is proceeding satisfactorily; hopes we are playing Monopoly or Scrabble, or whatever, to pass the time whilst the rain is pouring down.

August 22: Richard sends conveyance for us to sign in presence of witness. Expects completion on September 7.

August 24: Richard forwards legal charge for signing. Expresses concern that local authority have absolute discretion in variation of interest on mortgage, but adds that our only safeguard would seem to be that it is the local council and not some avaricious finance company. Asks for cheque for £576·40, being the balance between deposit and mortgage, plus legal fees.

September 6: Richard phones with news that purchase was completed the day before. First monthly payment of mortgage to the council is due on October 1 – £39·86 (it has already gone up since the offer made in June!). Keys, he adds, can be collected any time from the estate agents. He also encloses his firm's account – £85·75 – which is less that we expected. We pay up. The cottage is ours.

24

CHAPTER TWO

In which

we learn about our cottage

and the village in which it stands

My diary ended at the point of purchase, a suitably euphoric signing off. Reading it again reminded me how little we knew about our cottage in September 1973, although we had debated the minutiae of its purchase for nearly five months. So this is a chapter about the village of Wiggenhall St Germans and the history, as gradually we came to know it, of our cottage – an interlude before the narrative is resumed.

The village is one of a quartet with the Wiggenhall prefix and all within four miles of each other, the name referring to a Norfolk landowner from the Middle Ages. Immediately up river is Wiggenhall St Peter, with a ruined church nestling into the bank, a mile or two farther on is Wiggenhall St Mary Magdalen where the church has what is known as a 'weeping' chancel, slightly askew from the nave and thought by some to indicate the position of Christ's head on the cross. A third Wiggenhall, St Mary the Virgin, lies due west from St Germans.

The origin of our St Germans tag can be found in the church. The church, and the village, is named after St Germanus, Bishop of Auxerre and one of the most celebrated of the Gallican bishops. He was sent by the Council of Arles to England to oppose the Pelagian heresy which was then spreading rapidly, but which he checked by the eloquence and learning he brought to bear on the subject. He came to England a second time when the heresy was on the increase, and effectually subdued it, 'enlightening', according to one source, 'the whole Isle with the rays of his sanctity'. It is said that thirteen

25

The church at St.
Germans, an early
November morning.

churches still retain the dedication to his honour; Selby Abbey, for instance, is in the joint name of SS Mary and Germanus. Some writers give July 26 and others July 31 as the day on which he was commemorated. The date of St Germans' Fair is given as July 29, although it is many years since our village has celebrated the date with appropriate festivities.

There is also a legend associated with St Germanus: that being a young man with a large estate, and very fond of hunting, he hung the heads of beasts he killed on a pine tree in the middle of the town of Auxerre. Amator, Bishop of that See, cut down the tree which so enraged Germanus that he resolved to be revenged. In the meantime Amator had a vision which revealed to him that his death was near at hand, and that he who threatened his life was to be successor. He at once laid hold of Germanus, ordained him deacon, and informed him that he was to succeed as Bishop. As soon as Germanus recovered from his surprise, according to one account, 'God, who had directed the whole affair, so touched his heart that when upon the death of Amator, a few days after, he was chosen to succeed him, he made his life a model of the episcopal character.'

Thus, Germanus, in accordance with this legend, is represented in carvings on the bench ends of our village church as a Bishop with dead or hunted beasts lying around him. Nikolaus Pevsner in his *Buildings of Britain* * describes them as 'a good set'. The church contains many other delights – several old and rusting stoves with flues pushing up through the roof, and on the pulpit an hour-glass stand. But present-day parsons have watches and, as a notice by the pulpit states, the hour-glass is no longer used. A shame! But the upkeep of Norfolk's astonishing number and variety of churches (on a clear day we can see six from our river-bank vantage point) is increasingly a problem. My mother reported that a Harvest Festival service she attended at St Germans was punctuated by drips of rain-water falling into a tin bucket.

We first visited the church before our cottage had a proper name. You will recall that the estate agent's blurb referred to 'The Cottage, the Riverbank', indeed the solicitors from both sides and the Borough

* *Buildings of Britain: North-West and South Norfolk*, by Nikolaus Pevsner. London, Penguin, 1962

The hourglass on the pulpit,
St. Germans.

of King's Lynn all described it thus on their documentation. I toyed with the possibilities; we had to give it a name. But I soon gave up, mainly because my mind kept returning to a verbal pun that sprang to mind after one Sunday lunch: 'How about "Ouse Who"?' I suggested. But the family only greeted this with groans. We thought no more until a letter arrived from the post office, supplying us with a postcard, but that was not all: the letter was addressed to the 'Occupier, *Bank Cottage, Surrey Street*, St Germans'. A year later we even gained a number, five, from the Electricity Board. Not that all this nomenclature matters. In any village newcomers are swiftly identified, and St Germans was no exception.

Bank Cottage was an obvious and acceptable name, but what about Surrey Street? Rather grand, we felt, for an unmade-up cul-de-sac. In fact for some time afterwards I believed that we – the newest inhabitants of St Germans – were the only residents who knew that our street even had a name. Surrey Street is no more than twenty yards long, running at right angles between the river and the Central Stores where it opens out into what I felt must be called The Square or The Green, or something. Not long after we finally moved in, in 1975, workmen from the new West Norfolk District Council turned up, dug holes for concrete posts and installed metal nameplates. In an afternoon our street was not merely identified to the world, but also enlarged as the signs went up beyond the Central Stores and also outside the old post office on the other side and round the corner. But why *Surrey* Street? My mother discovered the connection: not twenty miles away the first Earl of Surrey in Norman times built Castle Acre and the second Earl founded Castle Acre Priory, the remains of which are one of the most impressive ruins in the Eastern Counties.

Wiggenhall St Germans is a large, even sprawling village, divided by the Great Ouse. The area round about is known as the Norfolk Marshland, although some authorities also tell you that the Ouse is the demarcation line between Marshland and High Norfolk. Bank Cottage and Surrey Street are on the east, or High Norfolk bank, as is most of King's Lynn, which is not just our nearest town, but also a thriving port and capital of West Norfolk. At Lynn, as it is known

The centre of St. Germans, fifty years ago and today.

locally, the Great Ouse is bridged twice as it runs into the Wash and, ultimately, the North Sea.

The centre of St Germans is a mixture of mainly eighteenth and early nineteenth century, although there are one or two older buildings. There should also be another terrace like ours but it was pulled down twenty years ago to be replaced by a garage and an engineering works. This terrace, unlike its successors, gave the illusion that the centre of St Germans was a square.

30

I have said nothing so far about the age of Bank Cottage and the Surrey Street terrace for one good reason – we don't know for certain as no two authorities have been able to agree. The suggestions have been many: architect, neighbours, public health inspector, district surveyor, the vicar in his role as local historian, all have had their say. The dates they offer range from 1700 to 1825. But there are clues.

Bank Cottage is at the river end of a terrace of what I took at first to be four cottages. There is a fifth house, at the other end, but this seemed to have been tacked on separately as its roof is far more steeply raked and two dormer windows pierce the old tiles, a delightful mixture of different types, sizes and colours. This house is called the Old Black Horse, and was until the beginning of the 1960s one of St Germans' many public houses (five in 1951, four in 1960, but only two today).

But I digress. The four cottages of the terrace, with their shallower raked roofs and matching clay pantiles are not quite what they seem from the outside. Before we rendered the end gable wall facing the river it was possible to see from the setting of the bricks that the roof appeared to have been raised at some date in the past. I was puzzled. Had our cottage been modernized (I use the word advisedly) before? The main clue can be found upstairs.

Waist high in one room and nearer my chest in the other, there is a ledge. We wondered why for many months, and then someone (I forget who) suggested the answer. A century or more ago here was where the roof began, not tiled as now, but thatched, and thatch needs a steeper run-off for rain-water. Later when tiles replaced the Norfolk reeds the walls were raised thereby improving the headroom upstairs. If this was so the old thatch might have contained dormer windows for first-floor rooms. Therefore it seems possible, even probable, that the Old Black Horse was originally part of the terrace, but didn't have its roof raised with the other cottages.

Again at quite an early date a previous owner decided to enlarge our cottage, which is now the largest. Originally it would have been as much a one-up and one-downer as the others, but in a smart move two rooms of similar dimensions were built at the back giving the cottage a

31

view west over the Ouse. Thus newcomers get the impression that our house is 'L' shaped, although this is only true by a matter of eighteen inches. I have two reasons for believing it was extended soon after the original; firstly, that it has the similar first-floor ledge, and, secondly, there is the evidence of the actual bricks with which it was built. As in the rest of the terrace they have a diagonal fault running down each face. Indeed the same bricks can be found on the other side of Surrey Street in Riverside Cottage, once the village alms-houses, and only converted two years before ours.

Since the beginning of the 1970s this corner of St Germans has seen extensive restoration. Not many years earlier the alms-houses had been auctioned in one of the village pubs and bought, derelict, for £50. As I write the three middle cottages of our terrace are waiting to be converted into a single home. The improvement will come not before time as one has a demolition order placed on it, and another a closure order. Taken as a whole our terrace seemed to me from the first to be an unassuming period piece. But round the back the relative order of the front became a chaos of assorted corrugated iron shelters, brick privies at the bottom of gardens, ramshackle fences. Our garden was almost totally covered by one vast shed. We also had a lean-to, pantiled outhouse with doors on both sides. In condition it was, remarkably, worse than the house. One door was impossible to open (and indeed I never did see its interior; by the time the lock was forced, the builders had demolished it). At the other end was what appeared to be a wash-house, although it lacked running water.

At the foot of our garden, apart from an outside lavatory, is a most imposing brick summer-house. In fact my eye was drawn to it in the

photograph on the front of the estate agents' literature. Sadly for us it turned out to belong to St German's Hall, a large house that is shielded from our view during the summer months by several chestnuts and a sycamore. Known locally as the Old Hall, it is described by Pevsner in his *Buildings of Britain* as:

> Facing the river. Late seventeenth century with Georgianized centre and two slightly projecting wings with stepped gables. Brick lintel stones, alternatingly projecting, brick modillion course. A square brick garden house with pyramid roof has brick quoins.

As befits a house a century older than ours it had already been restored when we first came to St Germans, but not by long. John Wallwork, the present owner, has told me that the roof was in an appalling state when he and his wife Ann bought the house, leaks having been plugged in places by the expedient of pouring on a slurry of cement. The roof rebuilt looks a treat and does the Wallworks great credit. But at the time we first saw the Old Hall they were not in evidence and were to remain a mystery to us for some time.

In the beginning we knew very little about the previous occupants of Bank Cottage, other than that we purchased it from the estate of Mr T.A. Emms ('Ah, you live in old Taggy Emms' house', said a man from the village with whom I got into conversation one day). Not long after we moved in, one of his relations, the lady who kept the keys when we first viewed the cottage, kindly gave us some of the papers relating to his purchase a quarter of a century before. According to these Thomas Arthur Emms bought two adjoining cottages for £500 in 1948 and immediately sold the one next door for £350. To secure the other, the one in which he was to live until his death, he took out a mortgage with the Prince of Wales Lodge of Oddfellows for £150. Thus it can be said that in twenty-five years the value of Bank Cottage appreciated over 3,500 per cent. Contrast this with the solicitors' fees. These in 1948 amounted to £15 17s 6d. In 1973 we paid £85.75.

We knew no more until just before the manuscript of this book was due to my publishers. Then for the first time we were able to sift through the deeds. Mr Emms, it turned out, already lived in Bank

34

Cottage before he bought it; in fact he had been a tenant since the early 'thirties. Through the legal documents we were able to trace the ownership back to the mid-1850s, when it had been the home of Anne Carter, widow. In 1868 it was in the hands of her 'direct lineal descendant', John Hardy Carter, who lived there until his death in January 1925. It is harder to trace prices as Bank Cottage always seemed to have been sold with some other property, but it was certainly officially valued at £250 before the Oddfellows granted Mr Emms his mortgage.

The interior of Bank Cottage was an astonishing sight to Londoners brought up in middle-class, semi-detached security. Once emptied of Mr Emms' possessions, it was difficult to envisage that anyone had so recently been able to live there. Used as we are today to cavity walls and damp courses (although we may be unaware of them) as well as central heating, it was still remarkable that a cottage so riddled with damp was actually habitable. In what passed for the kitchen/dining-room was, to quote the agents, 'a fitted range with oven and fireplace, storage cupboard and cupboard under the stairs, door to rear yard and side entrance porch. Electric cooker panel, power point'. As Sue was to remark: 'Who cares? No one is going to live in it in that state. They're going to tear it all out.' Indeed, but the range was to prove more important than its appearance suggested. On the floor we peeled up half a dozen layers of linoleum in various stages of decomposition and hiding a cracked and bumpy quarry-tile floor. 'It acts just like a wick, drawing the moisture into the room', said Mr Hurst, the public health inspector's man. The other downstairs room was similar, if worse. It had been the sitting-room, complete with the pianola. The plaster was sodden, but some rudimentary attempts at damp-proofing had been attempted with agricultural polythene bags underneath the wallpaper. Elsewhere – and this was no isolated case as I found the same in the cottage next door – the top wall covering when pulled away revealed newspapers of varying vintages used as lining paper underneath.

Although the original prospectus indicated that mains water was connected, a detailed inspection of the property failed to reveal so

much as a pump let alone a tap. Even in the lean-to at the back with its old cast-iron boiler, water was absent. Yet at an early stage, with the mystery unresolved, we received a water rate demand. It was then that inspiration dawned: the water supply served the outside lavatory, but nothing else. Meanwhile as we pottered around, getting to know our property, our next-door neighbour, Mrs Millie Dent, was still in residence. Her cottage suffered less badly from damp – it was the one that Mr Emms had sold for £350 – and she had a kitchen in a lean-to at the back, but the tiny staircase in the recess between the chimney breast and rear cottage wall would have frightened me each time I used it. She was the tenant and shortly to be rehoused.

Our cottage possessed two staircases, although as Mr Hurst had pointed out, neither complied with building regulations. Like Millie we had a recess staircase with an almost spiral tightness of tread. This was from the kitchen/dining-room to the bedroom at the back. From the front room downstairs ran a more modern straight flight into the bedroom above. But it was so steep that the only safe way of descending was backwards as on a ladder. The landing at the top was so shallow that it was almost impossible to stand on it without toppling over. It too could be used to reach the back bedroom, but to do so meant stepping back and up a further step as the floor levels were different.

The ceilings in the two upstairs rooms sagged alarmingly and showed signs of damp. 'They'll have to come down', said Mr Hurst. In fact when Ray Noyce, our builder and brother of our architect, set to work on the front room, a fog of dust descended, leaving behind in one corner a bird's nest of considerable proportions. I never heard which species was responsible, but it looked to my inexpert eye as if it had been added to year by year. As house martins return annually to nest under the bridge nearby, was it possible, I hoped, that they had adopted our roof, too? Certainly it would be no problem for them to fly in under the curved pantiles where they overhung the guttering (and sparrows soon found that the gaps between the new concrete tiles and the roof felt were also ideal nesting places).

In places it was evident that rising damp had reached the first floor and the front bedroom floor sagged alarmingly. Again linoleum was considered the cure-all, this time for decaying floor timbers, although

here we also have a second floor which had at some time previously been laid over the original, holes and all. This was only discovered when we removed the ceiling from the room beneath.

Although the house had only two downstairs rooms it did boast three outside doors. The original cottage door at the front of the terrace was seized solid. Around the side, nestling in a more recent addition, a porch, was the main door into the kitchen/dining-room, and at the back was a further door that led into the garden by a three-foot right of way. Alternatively, as no boundary fence existed, it was possible to take two strides and be knocking at Millie's back door.

Outside a climbing rose rambled, yellow but unidentified, accompanied by a mound of arabis against the lean-to, and a magnificent white perennial sweet pea that seeded itself extensively and which I hoped – forlornly as it turned out – might triumph again despite the excavations. Mr Emms, we soon learnt, had been a grand gardener. Indeed the landlady of the Crown and Anchor told us shortly before she retired, that his strawberries were the tastiest in the village. His secret, I imagine, died with him.

We learnt little more about the house. There were no interesting relics under the floorboards. A broken down old chest of drawers contained nothing but small items of junk, but was topped by an enormous, if pock-marked, old mirror which we always intended to have resilvered. Sadly this was not to be: it was destroyed in a gale during our first summer of occupation when parked temporarily outside. But as excavations went on Don Noyce, our architect, and the builders began to unearth the broken remnants of clay pipes. The stems became so common that we became quite blasé about finding so many, but the bowls were rarer. Don managed to reconstruct one or two, even dating some as early as 1690. Our own collection was paltry until our first Christmas, when on levelling a path outside I unearthed a perfect bowl at least two-hundred years old. This kind of archaeological evidence is certainly not proof in itself when dating the buildings nearby, but as our village sprang into prominence as far back as 1300, it is fair to assume, I think, that the site of our cottage – being so near the bridge – was built on at an early date and only followed later by our particular cottage, the terrace and the alms-houses opposite.

We knew little of this in September 1973. The first hurdle had been cleared. Now for the hard part.

CHAPTER THREE

In which

plans are formulated, landslides are prevented
and our local council cuts the red tape

Our euphoria was slow to die. It was a year since we first thought
seriously of the idea, but now a Norfolk cottage was ours, even if the
Borough of King's Lynn claimed an eighty per cent mortgage, even if
it did have a closure order on it from Downham Rural District
Council. Closure order? When this had first been mentioned I waved
an arm airily and thought little more, but now I rummaged through
our papers. There it was, and what a frightening document too, once
the legal jargon ('whereas this . . . perhaps that . . . ') was
deciphered. Cruelly précised it reads:

HOUSING ACT, 1957

Closing Order in lieu of Demolition Order in respect of a House.
'Downham Rural District Council being satisfied that the house
known as 'Bank Cottage', Surrey Street, St Germans, formerly
occupied by T.A. Emms (dec'd) . . . unfit for human habitation and
is not capable of being made fit at reasonable cost . . . inexpedient to
make a demolition order having regard to the effect of demolition
of the house upon other houses or buildings, now therefore the
council . . . by this order prohibit the use of the above-mentioned
house for any purpose.'

40

My first thought on reading that final sentence – not even chickens?

In fact during negotiations, Richard, our solicitor, had underlined just what we were letting ourselves in for. I looked up the relevant letter. The Borough of King's Lynn, in offering us a mortgage, itemized eight stipulations covering a sheet of quarto single-spaced. It was an awesome-looking list; had I really dismissed it so airily?

Yet nothing on it seemed unreasonable: damp-proof course, bathroom, hot water system, power supply, replastering, new window frames, redecoration, repointing. Dealing as we were with two local authorities, Richard asked Downham, who had been responsible for the closure order and from whom we were seeking an improvement grant, if the King's Lynn list was sufficient. As one might have expected, back came the reply that it wasn't; they also wanted the provision of 'adequate light and ventilation', which Richard pointed out was 'vague and general and could entail considerable expense, if for example it meant removing existing windows and putting in larger ones' (but we weren't going to stop now just because of the size of the windows), and secondly, the 'repair or removal of defective ceiling'. As all Bank Cottage's ceilings seemed to me to be defective this seemed not unreasonable.

But the Downham letter was also reassuring, and at this moment we needed all the reassurance we would get. 'Of course,' wrote G.S. Sennitt, senior public health inspector, 'all the items will be covered by the grant application; form and details of our local requirements are enclosed. Mr Hurst of this department would be pleased to meet your client and/or his architect at the house to discuss the grant etc.' Ah! Mr Hurst. As I have related, it was he who had been so helpful originally, meeting me off the London train, advising on renovations and recommending architects. It was Mr Hurst who told me about the county planning department's enthusiasm for the whole terrace, an enthusiasm that was to rebound on us fifteen months later; but that's another story. Meanwhile the county planners had 'expressed the hope' that our cottage and the two adjoining 'will somehow be preserved and the Council have been asked to see if anything can be done to this end'. A demolition order had actually been placed on the cottage immediately next to ours, which meant that Millie, the occupier, would have to be rehoused. Downham had taken this extreme course, because, they said, a closure order cannot properly be placed on occupied property. The middle cottage in the row, meanwhile, being unoccupied like ours, had got away with the less fearsome-sounding closure order. Ideally, I suppose, someone should have purchased all three. If only we had had the money we would have liked to have bought Millie's at least, thereby saving the need to add a kitchen/bathroom extension. We would also have gained, at least, an extra bedroom. But it was no good wishing; we didn't have the cash.

Although Mr Hurst had produced a list of architects in May it was not until the autumn and the cottage was actually ours that I looked at it again. He had underlined three whom he considered might best be suited to our needs. Of one he spoke with particular warmth ('I can understand his plans', I recall him saying.) Thus in September 1973 I rang Donald Noyce. He lived in Watlington, a neighbouring village across the railway line from us. I didn't know what to expect, but to my pleasant surprise he not only showed enthusiasm from the start, but like Mr Hurst was quick to offer to meet me off the London train at Downham, which he did the very next day.

We inspected Bank Cottage, discussed what I had in mind, and found within an hour that our ideas coincided. My main concern was to discover what such renovation might cost. Mr Hurst had suggested, in his rough and ready way, about £3,500, and to my relief Don concurred, although quite sensibly he added that this was the crudest possible estimate. That evening I discussed my favourable impressions with Sue and promptly wrote to Don confirming that we wished him to take on the job. I see, looking back at my letter, that I enclosed various documents relating to the cottage (not least the combined stipulations of the two boroughs), the information that mains drainage was due in the village in the following spring, and added that I would arrange for a second front door key to be cut. Don responded, stated that his fee would be 7½ per cent of the accepted builder's estimate, a percentage that seems to me in retrospect to have been a

42

With Don Noyce, our architect on the river bank.

bargain, considering all the work that he was to put into the job. He added that he hoped to make a start in November.

The first flush of excitement duly passed. Christmas came. One Saturday I drove my parents and Simon from London to see what we had bought. I think they were shocked (although they didn't show it) and wondered if we were going to be able to cope. Looking back I think they were right to be concerned. I often wonder if we would have dared to buy Bank Cottage – any cottage – if we had known what we were letting ourselves in for. Thanks be for the bliss of ignorance. Sue's mother also came to see the cottage. Apart from her much-voiced concern at our being so close to a river she had leapt ahead of us, as was her wont, and looked over the newly restored Riverside Cottage, on the other side of Surrey Street and immediately up river from us, and which she promptly suggested she should buy. What she was going to do for money we never learnt. She talked to the owner, a man of Kent who had undertaken the restoration as an investment, and discovered

43

that his bank manager was pressing him to sell and ease his overdraft. But like many of my mother-in-law's plans, they were glorious pipe-dreams and best treated, however gently, as such. Sadly she did not live to see work on Bank Cottage completed.

Don's first sketch plans were, as Sue remarked at the time, on what seemed like greaseproof paper. Downstairs consisted of the bathroom and kitchen extension, dining-room, plus two small bedrooms for the children carved from the existing front room; upstairs the sitting-room (*à la* Mr Hurst) and the master bedroom. Don suggested it would be more in keeping with the cottage if the extension had a sloping roof and pantiles rather than a flat roof in the manner of most such additions. We agreed. Sue's mother looked at the greaseproof sketch and made a suggestion that was to be the only major alteration to Don's plans: swapping round the sitting-room and the master bedroom: it was her absolutely spot-on reasoning that it would be less noisy in the children's rooms downstairs if our bedroom rather than the sitting-room was over them. Don went ahead, produced the scale drawings – which we gave the once-over – and application for planning permission was duly made. This was February 1974.

One original touch in the plans particularly appealed to us: Don linked the extension and the boundary wall by means of an arched gateway. It looked good on the plans and it looks good today in execution with honeysuckle ready to soften its lines. Don added carefully in his covering letter: ' . . . I thought if we had approval for this now, you could decide later if you would like this work carried out or not, without entailing a further planning application.' He added that he was submitting the application for a discretionary grant in time for Downham's next meeting, and that the Georgian-style windows he proposed were in keeping with the rest of the terrace and had in one room even been increased in size to meet Downham's stipulations (the extra cost had not, it turned out, been more than a few pounds).

But the biggest items in his covering letter concerned the river bank. Don suggested lowering the path around the cottage in order to help the damp problems. As this would mean interfering with the foot of the

44

bank it would have to be cleared with the formidable sounding body, the Great Ouse River Authority, and he had already arranged a meeting with the District Engineer. The plans would then be submitted to Downham. Only three days later he was writing to report on a 'very satisfactory discussion' with the District Engineer, who suggested adding a retaining wall at the foot of the bank to prevent any landslides onto the path. The one drawback was financial: the wall would add about £120 to our costs (a total as yet undetermined). But we weren't going to argue with the experts. In fact the District Engineer turned out to be a keen gardener too, as I shall relate in a later chapter.

In those days before the local government reorganization the council planning departments moved with commendable speed. For the purposes of the grant Don now estimated the total cost, as no builder's estimate was available. This came to £4,044·53, plus his professional fee which amounted to £303, although Don stressed that the final builder's estimate *could well be below that shown* (but no one was to realize that within a few months commodity prices were to rocket). Savings, he added, could be made if we were prepared to undertake any of the work ourselves, such as internal decorations (how perspicacious he was to prove). Don's final remark was much appreciated: 'Please let me know if the estimated cost of the work is wildly above what you are prepared to spend, so that I can consider what savings can be made.' Although the totted up figure of £4,347·53 seemed a large sum we would not have bought the cottage but for the knowledge that Sue had access to £3,000 from a family trust; add to this the £1,000 in discretionary grant money and we were almost there. Our building society and deposit accounts would be raided for the rest.

Three days later we received a letter from J.S. Bissett, clerk to the Great Ouse River Authority giving formal notice of consent to the river bank retaining wall. Hurrah! Four days on and Downham told us our grant was under consideration and could they have formal letters, first from our solicitor confirming that we owned the freehold, and secondly from the mortgagees consenting to the carrying out of the work. I wrote to each, but even before their replies had been

46

received came a further letter from Downham (dated just seven days after the first) actually giving us the grant. Hurrahs again! What had prompted such speed? Realization came swiftly. Downham Rural District Council would in one week's time cease to exist under the local government reorganization, to be superseded by a larger body to be known as the West Norfolk District Council. Obviously in their dying breath Downham were determined to hand over as little uncompleted business as possible. Indeed they also gave us planning permission that final week. We were to mourn their passing.

CHAPTER FOUR

In which
we learn the meaning of patience,
diagnose 'constructional indigestion' and
receive an electric shock

First the good news. Don's letter of April 8 informed us that all the building approvals had now been received. 'Unfortunately', he added, 'I have not been able to find a builder so far who is in a position to start the work in the near future.' We had been luxuriating in our success so far and to be stymied just as plans were ready to be translated into bricks and mortar seemed unfair. The lack of builders was a hangover from the notorious 'three-day week' of the previous winter. Every firm fell behind on its contracts and new work piled up.

Don had a possible answer. As he noted in his letter the difficulties he was experiencing in finding builders had led him and his brother Ray to form their own building company to carry out improvement work. 'We could undertake this contract in about one month's time if necessary, but I would in any case obtain competitive tenders from other builders.' We realized the difficult situation that might arise if Don was wearing two hats: as our architect (i.e. our agent) and also as our builder, but we were desperate to get the work started. Any hope that we might be able to occupy Bank Cottage that summer had long been abandoned, but if we didn't start soon, then next year would be in danger as well.

Another niggle at the back of my mind concerned a condition of our mortgage with the Borough of King's Lynn – that the renovation and improvement of Bank Cottage would be completed within nine months of purchase. Sure enough a month after Don had diagnosed 'constructional indigestion' there came an ominous sounding letter from the West Norfolk District Council, which had succeeded the old borough in the local government reorganization. It stated:

'This period [the nine months] has now expired and before arranging for an inspection to be made by the Council's Building Inspector, I shall be glad to know whether the works have actually been completed in accordance with your covenant in the Mortgage. If not please let me have an explanation for the delay and an estimate of the date when you anticipate completion of the works.' Signed J.H. Carr (District Secretary).

I replied that we too had hoped to have completed now, but – and here I blamed the 'three-day week' for all it was worth – no builder could be found who would or could undertake the contract. We were doing our best and hoped to begin shortly. Meanwhile I would get our architect to provide precise details of our predicament. To give Mr Carr his due, back came his reply three days later: 'In view of the circumstances . . . I am prepared to extend the period for completion of the repairs by a further six months . . . ' We blessed Mr Carr's reasonableness. Next day came a further letter from Don. He still had no estimates, but two builders had shown preliminary interest in doing the work and were prepared to quote. This in itself was a leap forward. But Don added a rider: 'Unfortunately prices are rising all the time in the building industry and I could not guarantee that the figures which I arrived at in February will still be correct now.' The oil-producing countries had pushed up prices, and timber, copper, lead, each soared almost by the week. It was all the more important it seemed to us, to get a builder, a reasonable quotation and a contract as soon as possible. I paid the first portion of Don's own account: for drawing up plans, getting planning permission, discretionary grant etc., which amounted to £222·22, or five per cent of the estimated contract price of £4,044·53, plus VAT. The rest of his fee, a further 2½ per cent, would follow on completion of the contract.

We echoed his final sentence: 'I hope to be able to report with favourable news in the near future'.

The news, when it came via Don's next letter on June 5, was hardly that. True, it included an estimate – for £4,479 as a result of 'your recent esteemed enquiry' – but, as Don noted, it did not appear to be a fixed price quotation ('this estimate is open for acceptance within one month, is subject to increases in labour and materials should they occur . . . '). Don queried the high price and was told that this was due to pay rises in the building industry from June 10 (believed to be £4·20 a week) 'and imminent further rises in material costs'. We turned it down.

We felt even more miserable when by the next post West Norfolk District Council informed us that the mortgage interest was about to rise – to 11½ per cent, or three per cent more than we had agreed to pay when taking out the mortgage nine months before. Inflation was upon us with a vengeance. In fact the second builder Don tackled ultimately declined to submit an estimate, being afraid to tie himself down to a fixed price, 'in view of the constant rise in material costs'.

I was beginning to wonder just how much more the next estimate might be. It arrived on July 1, the staggering sum of £4,964, which once again would be 'subject to any increases in labour and materials which may occur'. But the effects of the 'three-day week' appeared to be over. This builder was in a position to start within a week or two.

Don commented that 'in view of the apparent discrepancy between my original pricing of the work and the current building costs, I have re-estimated and find that prices have indeed risen over the last few months'. Thus he enclosed, 'for our information', an estimate from Heron Developments, the building company formed with his brother, which had just completed a contract for the Midland Bank in nearby Downham. The estimate, to my astonishment, considering that the previous ones had been for £4,797 and £4,964, was for a mere £4,680, although this was still more than £600 over his original estimate. We pondered. It was obvious we weren't going to get anything cheaper. Thus six days later, on July 7, I wrote accepting the Heron quotation.

50

The worst was obviously over; we were in the home straight . . . these were my thoughts at the time, but I should have known better as false dawns were already becoming a feature of the Bank Cottage saga. In my letter of acceptance I added that we would undertake the internal decorations ourselves (how much, I asked, would that save?) and as for the amount allowed for rewiring did this include a circuit for storage heaters?

Back came Don's reply. He would lop off £218 from the contract price for internal decorations, but the fitting of storage heaters raised a new problem. Apparently the electrical supply to our cottage (something described as single-phase, but which meant nothing to my non-electrical brain) would not bear more than a couple of storage heaters. The answer would be to have a new 'three-phase' supply laid to the cottage, if in fact such a supply was available in St Germans.

After all this we deserved some good news. And there it was at the foot of Don's letter. 'Heron Developments would be able to make a start on the work during the week commencing 22 July 1974. Unless I hear to the contrary before that date, I shall assume that this meets with your approval.' Not even all the electrical problems in north-west Norfolk were going to stop us employing a builder who could actually give us a starting date. Nearly eleven months after purchase we were finally under starter's orders.

CHAPTER FIVE

In which

Bank Cottage is reduced to a shell,
we say farewell to the porch, age another fifty years, and
offer up thanks for our privy

The builders' first act in restoring Bank Cottage was destruction.

We had decided the previous winter to holiday on the north Norfolk coast in the mistaken hope that by August building work would be near enough completion for us to take time off from the beach to begin decorating. Instead we drove from London at the end of July, the very week that Heron Developments began work. Making a detour via Bank Cottage on the way was only natural. We travelled via the west bank of the Ouse which meant that our first view of the cottage came as we topped St Germans bridge: nothing appeared to have altered. Turning off the road and parking in front of the Central Stores we looked up Surrey Street and the first sign of metamorphosis could be seen – against the front of the cottage was a stack of bricks sandwiching the odd wisps of straw.

I recall nothing else about that visit, but a fortnight later we drove across from Brancaster, where we were staying, and an astonishing sight greeted us: a yellow mechanical digger teetering on the edge of our river bank. Here was a point we had never considered: excavation of the path between the cottage and the river bank (as negotiated with the Great Ouse River Authority), demolition of the old coal- and wash-house, and the digging of the foundations for the extension; all this was fine in theory, but a major problem in practice which could be summed up in one word – access.

53

Sally Edwards, our neighbour across Surrey Street in Riverside Cottage, recalls that the builders tried first to manoeuvre the digger around the corner to excavate our path. But it was too tight for comfort with only inches between the digger and the Edwards' newly-built porch. Thus the digger on our bank, raised and tapering as it does for flood protection, and only just wide enough. In order to climb on to the bank the digger had first to carve a ramp from the road by the bridge, then back away in order to take a run at the slope (cheered on by the entire work-force of the garage nearby) before trundling the forty yards or so past the Edwards' house to ours. Torrential rain had been a feature of that August and soon turned the ramp into a quagmire, making the digger's progress more perilous than before. Next the builders' old lorry, for carting off the spoil, had to be dragged onto the bank top with the digger acting as winch.

'Many times I thought it was going to topple over into our garden. It was too frightening to watch', said Sally two years later, as we sat in the sun on that same bank, the digger's scars still discernible, and reminisced about those hectic times. We owe a lot to the Edwards' tolerance.

Despite every hindrance the excavation was completed. The lorry took seven trips to clear the rubble, although not all of it. A small mountain was to appear in our back garden as excavations for the sewer continued. It was ten months before its final hillocks were removed and only after Ray Noyce had suggested, more in hope than anything else, that it would make a 'smashing rockery'.

This was still in the future. The old coal and wash-house did not need much help from the demolishers before collapsing in a heap and a cloud of coal-impregnated dust. From the wash-house side we did rescue the old boiler which, although broken across its base, would, I felt sure, be serviceable one day in the future as an eccentric garden tub. I doubt that the other side had been used for years, because a substantial store of coal languished inside, under one of the staircases.

Rubbish began to accumulate. An old galvanized tank which used to take in rain-water from the Surrey Street side of the house, three doors, the remnants of the knee-high garden fencing, and as the roof

was stripped down, a pile of timber, much worm-eaten. The bank became a refuse tip for the detritus of the builders' occupation. Photographs in our albums show only the tip of the iceberg. As I garden on the bank today I invariably bring up chunks of brick, rusty wire, rotting wood fragments. Thank God the old paint cans, the cartons and the larger rubbish have long since been removed.

An immediate problem presented itself on our first official visit. While excavating the path the builders had been careful to negotiate the porch, which in Sue's view was one of the features of our cottage. Simply built in traditional cottage lines, with windows on either side, it was just the kind of addition that the city-dweller would expect, nay demand, to be covered by an undisciplined profusion of old roses, clematis and honeysuckle. It was a comparatively recent addition, being little more than forty years old (certainly not much more as I have a photograph from the 1920s which shows Bank Cottage without any such attachment). Although I approved of it in principle the bricks were ordinary flettons and the tiles untypical of the rest of the cottage. But excavating around it revealed that it had no foundations, being built straight up off the ground. Short of extensive and expensive underpinning it was bound to fall away from the house. Sue was heartbroken; the replacement Don reckoned at more than £100 which Sue felt we could not afford. But ultimately the sheer weight of masculine opinion decided the inevitable and the porch succumbed to demolition.

We were rapidly reaching the point where Bank Cottage was no more than a shell. Meanwhile our power crisis resolved itself. Don's electrical sub-contractor talked to the Eastern Electricity Board, which offered to supply us with the power we needed (including our off-peak storage heaters) for only £52·05. This included laying a new supply cable, and seeking a wayleave from the Edwards' across Surrey Street, as it had to come from the mains supply by the bridge. The only problem arose when the electricity board lost our file and I had to supply them with a copy of their original letter and estimate.

Gutting the cottage did reveal several curiosities. Most of the main roof timbers turned out to be in good condition, many being no more than roughly-shaped tree trunks, some even with scraps of the original bark attached (this is not as uncommon as I at first thought: a friend with a thatched cottage in Cambridge tells me that he has early seventeenth-century timbers in similar condition). It was at this point that Don told us that he had discovered that the party wall between Bank Cottage and Millie's next door, stopped at first floor ceiling level. This left us without a fire-stop in the roof. We wondered for a while whether to risk it, but common sense prevailed, even though it did mean one more addition to the final bill. The actual party wall, revealed when the plaster was hacked off, turned out to be timber framed, each square filled with bricks and rubble. Until then we had assumed that Bank Cottage was no more than 150 years old, but this kind of construction upset the theories and we began to refer to it proudly as 'late eighteenth century'.

Only a few weeks after we had bought the cottage, almost a year before, we received a letter from Downham Rural Council informing

56

us (to our pleasant surprise) that they would soon be connecting us to main drainage. It wasn't put as simply as that (it never is in council language):

> Notice is hereby given that the said Council in pursuance of the Public Health Act, 1963, section 42, intend to fill up the cesspool and do any work necessary for that purpose, first providing in a position equally convenient to you a drain or sewer equally effective for the drainage of the premises and communicating with a public sewer . . .

And here came the bit we liked best –

> . . . and that the said works will be performed at the expense of the said Council and will be commenced on the 29th October 1973 (or as soon as possible thereafter).

All of which was lovely, except that this was now August 1974. So Don contacted the council and was told, I think to his surprise, that we could be connected whenever we liked. We had wondered where the sewer would be laid and were told that the Council proposed to take it along the back of our terrace. Don also learnt that connection was only free to those cottages that actually had proper lavatories. Ours was in the garden, but that was good enough. Otherwise a charge would have been made, which as Don remarked 'seemed an odd sort of distinction to make, but in this case much more preferable than having fairies at the bottom of your garden'.

Praise be for our privy!

CHAPTER SIX

In which
building begins, we receive an objection,
a sewer is mislaid by 'half a bubble', we uncover
eighteenth century jerry-building, our water system gets wind,
and the Department of the Environment takes an interest

Everything began to happen so quickly. Only a month after work started Don was writing to us, 'I trust on your next visit a considerable improvement will be seen' and a week later, 'foundations have now been cast for the extension and river bank retaining wall, and brick-laying will commence on Monday 2nd September. The re-roofing of the house should be carried out in the next couple of weeks.'

I used to travel from London at least once a fortnight to see the progress for myself and discuss any problems that had arisen since each previous visit. It was possible to catch the first train from Liverpool Street, breakfast handsomely as we sped through Hertfordshire into Cambridgeshire, and marvel every time at the splendour of Ely's great cathedral. Repair work was being carried out on this too, which I found strangely reassuring. Each time I travelled up to Norfolk I would notice progress at Ely and wonder if it would be matched at Bank Cottage; each evening on my return I would judge who was winning this private race.

In mid-September *The Times* was running a correspondence about richness in place-names. Dorset had claimed itself king with Piddle-trenthide et al, when a reader from Ely chimed in:

58

The Fens possess not only the mellow Barcastrian (Swaffham Prior; Stone-cum-Quy), but also the confounding Wodehousian (Wiggenhall St Peter, Wiggenhall St Germans, Wiggenhall St Mary the Virgin and Wiggenhall St Mary Magdalen within a two mile radius). They offer pronunciation problems (Isleham; Quanea) and surprises (Friday Bridge; Queen Adelaide), but can boast the poetic (Chittering, Prickwillow, Wormegay, Guyhirn, Ring's End and Barton Bendish). Of course if it comes to a knock-down and drag-out affair, Sir, we shall put one blow in first with Snoot's Common and Grunty Fen.

I do not know how often the Wiggenhalls had made *The Times*, but never before, I wager, all on one day. I felt as proud of our newly-adopted village as if I had lived there all my life.

We had begun an album of photographs, and each time I look at them I am astonished afresh at how rapidly the pictures changed in these early days. Once the slabs for the extension and retaining wall were laid the new walls appeared to rocket into place. By October the cottage had its new roof, with enough old clay pantiles saved for the

Surrey Street frontage, but modern concrete ones for the rest of the roof and the extension.

It was too much to hope that we would get away unscathed. All the same it was surprise born out of innocence with which I greeted a caller who, put through to me at my office in *The Times*, asked if I owned a cottage in Norfolk, at St Germans. I only had to say that this was true, for the caller, a householder of the village, to let fly: did I realize that the builders were ruining our cottage? Modern bricks and concrete pantiles had no place on a cottage as interesting as ours: indeed the whole terrace should have had a preservation order years ago. In fact the County Council had been dragging its feet; the matter was now with the Department of the Environment, from whom we would shortly expect to hear.

Sue and I were aware of the County Council's interest, which was why we had built the extension with sloping roof, rather than flat. There had been that letter from Downham Rural Council some months before informing us that the county planners had 'expressed the hope' that our cottage and the two adjoining 'will somehow be preserved'. As for the roof we could have re-roofed it completely in concrete pantiles (or corrugated iron for that matter). Instead we decided to restore the front with the best of the original pantiles in order that it should be in keeping with the rest of the terrace; we wanted people to look up Surrey Street and see the cottages as a whole.

The Department of the Environment were certainly stung into action. It wasn't long before the West Norfolk District Council, acting as their representatives, sent a posse of officials to inspect what we were doing, presumably to report back to London before any final decision on whether or not our cottage, indeed the entire terrace should be listed. We were worried at first that all work of renovation might be stopped, but Don was reassuring. Planning permission had been given and it would be a costly business for the council to have it rescinded.

The specialist tradesmen who began working on our cottage were all sub-contractors, and to our surprise, there was hardly a man among them who was local. The Noyce brothers, Don and Ray, both

60

came to Norfolk from south of the Thames. The tiler and bricklayer both knew Highgate in north London where we had our flat. In fact the bricklayer had worked on a high-rise block not half a mile away before moving to Norfolk and running a village shop. But times for small shopkeepers being hard he returned to his trade. Similarly the plasterer, 'the best in Norfolk' as Don described him. He ran a pub for a time, but there wasn't sufficient money in it and he had gone back to plastering.

Meanwhile West Norfolk District Council were living up to the promise of the old Downham Rural Council over the sewer. As Don recalls, the job was done by a pleasant Irishman, 'obviously skilled in the art of drain laying' who laid the new sewer extension into the rear garden ready for the drains from the kitchen/bathroom. Once begun the work was carried out with remarkable speed and efficiency. Our builders left the Irishman to his task, while the brickwork to the new extension was being laid up to damp-proof course level.

Even before the brickwork mortar started its initial set, the new sewer was installed, the old cesspool was filled in, and the trenches back-filled. The Irishman departed. The time had now arrived for our builders to set out the new drains to serve the kitchen sink and the bathroom services. A 'Quickset' level was used to ensure that a gradient of at least 1 in 40 was obtained, to comply with the building regulations. To his dismay, Don found the extension floor level would be twelve inches too low, or more specifically, the newly-laid sewer was twelve inches too high. No wonder that Don remarked, 'with the sewer too high for the new drains and the old cesspool no longer in existence, a gloom settled on the proceedings'.

After the initial shock had passed, helped on by the builders' assorted curses directed, says Don, 'mainly at the Romans for their part in the invention of drainage', it was decided to explore the possibility of lowering the new sewer while still maintaining a gradient which might possibly be acceptable to the council. Don's 'Quickset' level was again set up and the sewer exposed where it first entered the premises and at its highest point – the open end on to which the new drains were meant to connect by means of a manhole.

Inspecting the new drains with Hubert Gorbould, who has just produced plans to restore the cottage next door.

Our builders were incredulous: in a matter of 32 feet, the sewer had been set to fall 1' 9½" – a gradient of 1 in 18, compared with the gradient required by the council of 1 in 40, a fall of 9½". Hence the missing 12".

Don advised the council of this and the genial Irishman returned, complete with new drain sections, connections and shovel. The situation was explained to him and he even seemed quite interested in the 'Quickset' level. When asked the gradient at which he thought the sewer had been laid, he looked puzzled and explained that he had set the drainpipes to 'half a bubble' on his spirit-level and that 'it should have been alright'.

The first sewer still exists across the garden, some feet down. The second sewer was laid anew, alongside the first and connected into the manhole on the adjacent property. Thus the outside lavatory at the

62

bottom of our garden, our surprising golden asset that ensured the connection to mains drainage free of charge in the first place, now had its own sewer. So too does the kitchen and bathroom extension. And neither cost us a penny.

Our regular visits saw considerable progress. The builders dug out the existing ground floors, replacing them with concrete slabs, substantially waterproofed. Getting on for eighteen months before, when we were negotiating for Bank Cottage I had obtained one estimate for a damp course that meant injecting silicones into the brickwork. Don, in an effort to save cash while maintaining standards, found a second firm which, despite inflation, was able to offer a quotation of £40 less, plus a twenty-year guarantee.

The old sash windows of varying types and sizes were ripped out and Georgian casement designs substituted. These, being of a larger window area gave us more light and seemed in keeping with the cottage and its period. Two of the river frontage windows were entirely new. The smaller of the two, to give light to the new stairs, proved simple enough. Ray rigged up some Heath Robinsonian scaffolding consisting of oil drums and a sloping plank to the top of the riverbank. The second window, to give more light and a river view from the master bedroom, showed just how haphazard building must have been two hundred years ago. At what was to be window-sill level he dug out a substantial piece of timber, a branch in perfect condition, but for a small rotten patch at the base. We pondered for a while and then realization dawned. Here was further evidence that the cottage had been thatched, the branch being left behind when the roof was raised.

We had always thought that jerry-building was the prerogative of the builders who put up what Alan Jackson, in his book of the same name, has called 'Semi-Detached London' * between the two world wars. But the installation of the windows at Bank Cottage proved that jerry-building existed two hundred years ago too. When Don first surveyed the cottage he pointed out a settlement crack on the Surrey Street frontage. Shortly before Christmas 1974, a public health inspector visited the site and also expressed concern. Wrote Don at the

* *Semi-Detached London*, by Alan Jackson. London, Allen & Unwin, 1974

63

Window contrasts: the Georgian casement for the sitting room (above); the new opening for our bedroom with the branch still in place (below) and the scene after brickwork had fallen away when the old sash frame was removed (right).

time: 'As you will know we have already allowed a sum for making good defective mortar joints and we hope that the crack may be satisfactorily corrected within this work.' And he added ominously as it turned out: 'The extent of settlement will not be entirely determined until broken bricks are removed.'

How right he was: the windows on this wall were the last to be renewed. As one of the old frames was pulled out so a substantial portion of old brickwork collapsed, too. What remained would never have passed building regulations today: broken bricks, rubble, lumps of clay, in fact anything that would fill a hole. Rebuilding the brickwork added another £40 to our bill.

It was hardly surprising, therefore, that the builders were finding what Don described as 'definite evidence of water penetration through the old brickwork'. In some areas clay seemed to have been used as a substitute for mortar. For a long time we dickered over the best way of coping with the exterior walls. When Mr Hurst first pointed out the defects to Bank Cottage he made it clear that not only would repointing be necessary, but in many places we would probably have to replace whole bricks which over two centuries had lost the battle against the elements. We were keen to keep the brickwork if possible, at least at first, but our conviction gradually weakened. Soon after Christmas Don made it clear that in his view only a waterproof cement render would entirely solve the problem. As long as we could look like the exterior of cottages at the other end of the terrace we were prepared to sacrifice the brickwork. Therefore at the beginning of January 1975 Don wrote to the council seeking approval.

The dining-room had a range, or, as you will recall from the estate agent's verbiage quoted earlier, 'a fitted range with oven and fireplace'. In an un-thought-out sort of way – there were, after all, more important things to think about – we muttered vaguely to ourselves about keeping it. Meanwhile the builders cast the dining-room's new floor, and only then did Sue, on a flying visit, realize that retaining this range was ridiculous. We wouldn't need it for heating as storage heaters would take care of that, nor would she expect to use its oven with an electric cooker installed in the new kitchen. But ordering the old stove's removal was one thing, actually doing the deed was quite another. As soon as the builders began to yank it from its long-held position than the chimney-breast began to move too. None of us realized just how important the 'fitted range' was to the cottage: in the absence of a beam the range was supporting the entire chimney-breast from floor to loft. Props were therefore rapidly inserted to avoid a calamity. The chimney itself was thick with soot. In some places it was possible to push my index finger right into the brickwork behind. In fact this brickwork turned out to be structurally unsound and ultimately had to be rebuilt. Don prepared a number of designs. We chose the simplest, which has given us a small inglenook recess, where once the 'fitted range' did its Charles Atlas act.

It was at about this time that we ended the small saga of the water supply. I have recounted previously how the search for the mains ended when we discovered that it surfaced only at the bottom of the garden – in the lavatory cistern. Don therefore approached the Anglian Water Authority seeking access to the main, only to be told that the nearest source whence a supply could be tapped was by St Germans bridge outside the old antiques shop which Sally Edwards had recently turned into The Riverside Gift Shop. That was the bad news, but worse was to follow: their charge for a new supply from this site would be over £100. Not surprisingly we chose the alternative: picking up the supply that served the outside lavatory, a job that would cost us only £20. Don warned that the pressure was lower than normal, but that it ought to be adequate for our needs. We were not thinking of installing a washing machine were we? The answer was 'No', not least because St Germans, ever full of surprises, has its own launderette. He also thought that possibly the storage tank would fill up rather more slowly than usual.

In this Don was correct, too correct, if that were possible. Six months went by before we experienced the sequel to this remark. Our first guests at the cottage, once it became habitable (although not finally completed) the following summer, were our close friends the Askews. Tony, as I shall relate later on, accompanied me almost every weekend when decorating was our priority, and he painted and paper

66

hung most expertly. But during this particular fortnight in July they were also the cottage's guinea-pigs. It would have been remarkable if there had been no snags. But the Askews turned on the water one day only to find that nothing emerged from the tap. Tony, who is a talented do-it-yourselfer, examined the system and diagnosed an air-lock. He phoned us, we phoned Don, and not long afterwards Ray turned up. Tony's diagnosis was correct and soon water was running again. Was this an isolated attack of wind? Should the patient receive further treatment, or even – and we crossed our fingers – would major surgery be necessary? Ray preferred to wait and see. Again an air-lock occurred. Tony and Ray between them reckoned that if the hot and cold bath taps were turned on full the low pressure supply was unable to fill the tank sufficiently quickly. Thus the tank in the roof emptied, air was drawn into the downpipe, and the air-lock developed.

Ray's answer was to double our cold-water storage. I had visions of taking down the bathroom ceiling (the tank is in the extension roofspace) in order to manhandle a large galvanized replacement into position. I was quickly corrected. These days cold-water tanks look more like plastic dustbins. Thus they can be squeezed through the average size loft trapdoor, which is, in our case, in the airing cupboard immediately above the hot-water tank. It was a sweltering day in July. Ray sweated enough perspiration to fill one of the tanks. To do the job he had drained the existing tank and turned off the mains supply, which meant that he expected to cause an air-lock in the process. But water systems are certainly never logical. We turned on the mains, filled up the tanks and then tried the bathtap. There was a whoosh and suddenly, with much spluttering, out poured the water; the sheer weight of two tankfulls had been enough to push the air-lock through the system and out into our bath. Another problem solved!

But I have leapt on six months. By Christmas, timbers in the cottage had been treated against furniture beetle and a twenty-year guarantee issued. Progress generally had, however, been slowed by the appallingly wet weather and lack of lighting as it was only the week before Christmas that the electricity board turned up, and then just to provide a temporary supply. This had delayed our electrical sub-

67

contractor and he only began wiring the cottage after Christmas. Don's end-of-year report noted that the new timber staircase was now fixed in position, that the partitioning around the stairwell was complete, that the floor had been made good across the opening where the recess staircase from the dining-room had been. With the extension roof completed the doorways from the dining-room into the kitchen and bathroom had now been formed.

Don looked ahead into the new year and forecast that plastering would begin in mid-January and take approximately two weeks. Plumbing and drainage work would then follow, as would the fixing of doors and skirtings, and further sundry work. After this only the finishing trades would remain outstanding. I was beginning to feel excitement welling up. I knew I could take a week off in mid-February and wrote to Don suggesting that if all went well I would spend a week camping out at the cottage to begin painting. With luck I thought we could be in occupation by Easter.

But it was not to be. Once again I allowed my optimism to run riot. By January 15 Don was writing to say that although he would do everything possible to have the house ready for my proposed decorating stay, he feared that the plaster might not be fully dried out, particularly if water penetration through the external walls existed to any extent. Three weeks later he confirmed his fears. 'The walls which were first plastered two/three weeks ago are still damp. The problems of penetrating damp through the external walls are now very apparent . . . the present spell of damp weather has served to aggravate the problem, especially in view of its proximity to the river.'

I postponed my visit.

As it happened, I would have done so anyway. In mid-February Sue's mother died in hospital after a short, but rampant illness. She had gone down horrifyingly fast. Every other emotion and consideration apart I was particularly sad that she would not see the restoration completed. If it hadn't been for her help in releasing funds from family trusts we would have been hard pressed to undertake the Bank Cottage adventure.

As if to take our minds off the bereavement, Don wrote on February

68

19 with important news. He had telephoned the council to seek news of our application to render the exterior walls, having heard nothing for six weeks. Their delay in replying was soon explained. Apparently our house and the rest of the terrace were to become listed buildings. Thus our rendering application was on ice until the Department of the Environment listing became official. There would be no question now of rubber stamping our application to let rendering commence. We would have to bide our time, but what we didn't realize, was for just how long.

CHAPTER SEVEN
In which
the Department of the Environment confirms its interest,
the word patience takes on new meaning, and
eleven months on
we count the cost of preservation

My emotions at Bank Cottage being listed as a 'building of special architectural or historic interest' were mixed. It was pleasant to think it justified the accolade, yet Sue and I couldn't help laughing at what had been listed. As a result of our renovation little of the original Bank Cottage remained apart from the basic brickwork and timbers in the roof and first floor. Indeed I still wonder what we could justifiably describe as 'original'. As I mentioned in an earlier chapter I have always taken the view that Bank Cottage has seen several 'modernizations' in its two hundred years' history. Internally all sorts of minor alterations took place, although one massive pine beam remains in our dining-room. Don and I never did satisfy ourselves over one curiosity: the rafters in the roof space above our sitting-room were painted white up to a certain height, making us wonder if the ceiling had once been higher.

So what were the Department of the Environment listing? One might say that Bank Cottage is a good example of the development of a Norfolk terraced cottage over two hundred years. But would it not have been better to have listed the building before our restoration began? Certainly we would then have been restricted in our plans, although I would defend to the last concrete pantile what we have

done. But Bank Cottage is now a *modernized* cottage. Listing it simply detracts from the point of the Department of the Environment's list.

The other viewpoint is that we should have placed the accent on *restoration*. Although if we had had the money I am sure we would have scoured Norfolk – England if necessary – for second-hand clay pantiles, about bricks I am less certain. It is, after all, difficult to determine which *are* the originals, but if our purse had been capacious enough no doubt we would not have rested until the precise match for our extension had been found (although even this would have had its problems; the range and variety of bricks used in the original cottage was enormous. Which ones would we have chosen?). But economic facts could not be ignored. We chose to render the exterior walls to keep out the damp, which in itself makes any concern for matching bricks irrelevant as the originals are all covered up. Our approach to Bank Cottage was a necessary compromise, born out of a desire to complete the work in time to satisfy the West Norfolk District Council and at a price we could afford, while at the same time doing it in a way that satisfied both our tastes and our consciences.

The first news about the listing had come from Don in mid-January, but it was not until mid-April that the bureaucratic D o E machinery cranked out a stencilled letter, with our address scrawled in, informing us of the Secretary of State's decision, but little else, except that details would follow from our local council. These duly appeared three weeks later with a covering letter signed by the District Secretary. We were informed that the D o E's lists are compiled 'on the expert advice of an expert committee of architects and historians'; that we need do nothing unless we proposed 'at any time to demolish the building or do any works (either to the exterior or to the interior) which would affect its character' – which we did, as rendering the cottage must affect the character of the exterior.

The letter had the answer: 'in that event you will need to seek "listed building consent" from the local council.'

There was even a paragraph about appealing against the decision actually to list the building. All you had to do was to write to the Secretary of State claiming that the building, your building, was 'not in fact of special architectural or historic interest . . . Any such claim, with the evidence to support it, will be carefully considered'. We toyed with the idea, but assumed it would take years, thereby hindering our application for planning permission for the rendering, except that it was now described as 'listed building consent'. And any delay in rendering would, we felt, have a detrimental effect on the fabric of the very building we were all eager to see renovated.

The official letter included a 'Guide to the Legislation'. I had not previously realized that it was D o E policy to list all pre-1700 buildings which survive in anything like their original condition. Additionally most buildings from 1700 to 1840 are listed; between 1840 and 1914 admission to the lists gets tougher, standards of character and quality being taken into account. The paragraph concluded: 'A start is now being made on listing selected buildings of 1914 to 1939.' At least that didn't affect us. Age is by no means the only criterion. I imagined, as I studied the possibilities (' . . . illustrating social and economic history . . . technological innovation or virtuosity . . . association with well-known characters or events . . . ') that we as a terrace had been included because of our 'group value, especially as examples of town planning: for instance, squares, terraces, or model villages'. But in our case, although we come into the 1700 to 1840 bracket, we are invalidated, surely, because we are no longer in anything like the original condition?

I suppose our emotions would have been less mixed if we hadn't wished to render Bank Cottage. In fact if we had applied only a few weeks earlier, permission would probably have been granted because West Norfolk District Council would have been unaware of the D o E's intentions. As it was we had wasted four months while the council put our application on ice. Finally with the listing confirmed, Don made formal application one day after the dating of West Norfolk's official letter of notification to us. We assumed that the matter might take three or four months at most to decide, and that we would still be able to do the job in late summer, or at worst in autumn before the warm, dry weather broke.

Four weeks later West Norfolk, as they were required to do, published notice of our application. On moving day we found a copy stuck to one of our Surrey Street windows. By then the statutory three weeks in which objections could be made were nearly up. The actual notice now resides in volume two of our photographic record.

Our intention to render also figured in a list of planning applications in the *Lynn News and Advertiser*. We wondered who would see it and waited with some trepidation. Certainly we knew there would be no objection from the Edwards across the way, nor from Hubert Gorbould, who ran a haulage firm and a string of gravel pits and had his own plans to convert the three middle-terrace cottages into one. He, too, wished to render his Surrey Street frontage in the manner of the Old Black Horse at the far end from us. That the Black Horse should have been rendered seemed to us the best possible support for

the Trewin, and later, the Gorbould application. It was, after all, in the most original condition of all cottages in the terrace, at least on the exterior, having not had its roof raised. I took detailed photographs of our brickwork showing how the facings had in many cases been consumed by the elements. The summer passed. Periodically Don asked the council what was happening, only to be told that 'our application was still under consideration'.

Towards the end of October we spent a week at Bank Cottage. It wasn't long after we arrived that we heard, to our dismay, a rumour that our application had been turned down. We inquired further; happily the rumour applied only to a possible committee recommendation: our application had still to go before the proper council meeting, probably a fortnight or so later. We held our breath and waited for Don to bring us news. It came in the post on November 18, but as we had come to expect in these matters it was not cut and dried. Don's letter gives the precise flavour:

'I spoke to the council on Friday and was told that their decision on the rendering had now been passed on to the Secretary of State for his comments. The person I spoke to at the council was unable to let me know the outcome of their meeting, but helpfully advised me that a refusal of our application would not have necessitated any communication to the Secretary of State. I was further informed that a final decision by the Secretary of State will be received within 28 days. Further delays unfortunately, but at least we do know the Council is on our side.'

A month later – on December 20 – we had the best Christmas present one could imagine. The Secretary of State for the Department of the Environment had approved our application. Don re-estimated the cost of the job – £246, or £78 more than his original estimate a year previously (most of the increase coming from a rise in scaffolding hire charges). Once Ron, the plasterer, was free, and all danger of frost passed, the work would be done.

I think our only concern was the final appearance of Bank Cottage. In our heart of hearts we would both have preferred to keep the brickwork. We knew that the cement screed would completely alter the appearance, but as I have said we felt there was no alternative. We had penetrating damp through the brickwork on the river frontage and it was Don's considered view, and later confirmed by West Norfolk District Council, that rendering was the only certain cure. One villager who showed concern feared that Bank Cottage would, in a damning phrase, end up 'looking like a council house'. I reassured him. I think he had visions of us ordering a Tyrolean finish, that frosted effect which is the 'seventies' equivalent of pebbledash. If penetrating damp was the problem, he asked, why didn't we use one of the transparent silicone waterproofers, having carefully repointed first? I responded that we all felt the brickwork was in too bad a condition for this; many of the brick-facings had been worn

away completely by the combined action of rain and salt-charged wind and spray from the tidal Ouse alongside. Cutting out and replacing these bricks – and there were many of them – would be an expensive business. What we had in mind was a flat render which we would paint, probably white, although not necessarily so, to match the Black Horse.

It had taken seven months for the council to make up their minds thanks mainly to the preservation complication. If only they had shifted themselves sooner we could have done the job in the autumn, thereby saving two nasty patches of penetrating damp revealing themselves during the winter in the master bedroom. In fact if our cottage hadn't been listed by the Department of the Environment none of this planning rigmarole would have been necessary. We would have been allowed to go ahead unhindered. The cottage would have benefited. And so, too, would our bank balance. Nor would it look a tile, brick or window frame different from what it does today.

We did have one seal of expert approval. Ever since I had first written about Bank Cottage in *The Times*, our activities had been closely followed by the Norfolk Archaeological Unit. Thus it was cheering to find a card in our letterbox from their Mr Edwin J. Rose: 'Called to inspect progress! Very good!'

CHAPTER EIGHT

In which
I camp out in Bank Cottage,
colours prove deceptive, snow stops play,
friends rally to the cause of decoration and
completion seems in sight

In devoting a chapter to Bank Cottage's official preservation I have leapt ahead in time. Back in the late winter of 1975, Don, Ray and company were trying to claw back the hours and weeks lost through the appalling autumn weather and the electricity board's sloth. Meanwhile I was itching to begin decorating. It was not a case of the builders moving out one evening in order to allow me to open paint tins next morning. Rather I foresaw that several weeks of good-natured cohabitation would be necessary. Thus in Easter week, just two years since I had first viewed the cottage, I took a week's holiday from *The Times* and drove up from London with a boot loaded with paints, food, a camp bed, sleeping bag, blankets, electric fire, hot water bottle, radio and substantial torch. I had come prepared for privation, but had no idea just how basic camping out in St Germans was going to be.

I suspect that Don thought me unhinged, or at best, a mite too keen. Although upstairs work was all but complete there were plenty of unfinished details. The ceilings had been renewed with plaster-board, but the joists were still visible. The plans mentioned an 'Artex' finish which meant nothing to me, but when Don explained that it is 'a plastic compound which is applied to the plaster-board

and treated to produce a stippled finish', I nodded sagely. It was the end of his sentence that gave me greatest pleasure: 'a stippled finish *that does not require decoration afterwards*' [my italics].

We had yet to make up our mind what to do about the sitting-room floor upstairs. The boards had been extensively patched, not least in the north-west corner where once the twisting recess stairs had emerged, but much of the rest was still full of holes, and dangerous. The room contained a standard Victorian cast-iron fireplace, which we ordered to be left. Sue, who has a feeling for antiques, or merely other people's junk, visualized it with the rust removed and the cast-iron treated with stove-black. Ron plastered carefully around it, but we still felt it needed a frame or something to set it off. As far as decorating was concerned – and that was, after all, why I was camping out at the cottage – I realized that I would have to concentrate on upstairs and the smaller of the two bedrooms on the ground floor. But the dining-room and the extension were still in chaos. Bags of cement, drain-piping, window frames for the porch, timber to complete the skirting and other minor joinery, masses of tools, paint and rubble.

To lessen my hardship, Don and Ray leant me an ancient Calor gas stove, but electricity was limited by the nature of the temporary supply: about three kilowatts, which I was told, amounted to an

electric fire, a couple of lights and my electric drill. I had one long extension lead, unsatisfactorily joined with insulating tape. Twice I tripped, pulled the joints apart in the process and fused the system. The torch proved its worth like no previous torch I have owned. But the worst privation was the lack of running water. True there was a tap in the neighbouring garden at the back, but when you have been brought up with h & c basin, bath and – as estate agents' blurbs are inclined to say in these parts – flush toilet, the total lack of such facilities is not merely annoying, it seems basically medieval. In fact from the other side of Surrey Street, Bob Edwards, arriving back from a trip that evening, remarked to his wife on seeing one of Bank Cottage's rooms lit: 'They haven't moved in already?' Perhaps I exaggerate. There was still our lavatory at the bottom of the garden, but despite the council's provision of two sewers, flushing proved most unsatisfactory, not to say unhygienic, thanks to some subterranean blockage. In the end I took to visiting King's Lynn daily, and using the Duke's Head, a splendid Trust House, in the Georgian Tuesday Market Place. I paid for the privilege, or salved my conscience – to my own satisfaction at least – by always downing a pint of their best bitter afterwards.

I started work the first evening of my arrival, which was a mistake. Among the cans of paint were several of undercoat. In the poor artificial light provided by one 60-watt bulb hanging insecurely from a bent nail I began with the windows. Now these are known as Georgian style and in the sitting-room, with the largest spread of window, we have twenty-four separate panes of glass, each encased in a wooden frame. Care and patience in abundance are necessary if one is to avoid too much paint on the glass. I soon ran out of both, and sloshed away. The sitting-room done, I moved onto the landing and then into the master bedroom. Nearly three hours and fifty-four panes later I fell back satisfied at my evening's labours and adjourned to the pub for refreshment. Having returned, organized my sleeping accommodation, boiled a kettle on the Calor gas stove (it took at least twenty minutes) and filled my hot-water bottle, I went to bed. I should have slept soundly – the reward for my labours. Instead I awoke in the small hours, cold and stiff – my sleeping bag must have been designed for a dwarf, being unable to accommodate me above my chest. I dozed the rest of the night and rose at dawn. At first it failed to register, but then the truth broke through my sleepiness: in the harshness of bright daylight the woodwork – all those Georgian windows – which I thought I had painted in a white undercoat, now greeted me in a dull yellow. I looked unbelieving and more carefully at the can of paint, which I should have done the night before. 'Undercoat for Canary Yellow' it stated boldly. I postponed further thought and set my mind to producing a breakfast that would take my mind off the disaster. At that moment there was a knock at the front door, where polythene sheeting still did service for glass, and a boy asked if I would like a cup of tea. I remember saying 'No' which, in retrospect, was ridiculous. I felt afterwards that I had been unnecessarily rude to Alan, the Edwards' son, but in my moment of truth I wanted to be alone.

Don, Ray and Ron arrived within a few minutes of each other as I was tidying away the breakfast things, or rather stacking them on what would become the dining-room window-sill, the only uncluttered shelf-space I could find. It was a question of what to do next. I could see the builders wanted something to get their teeth into, and after some discussion, we decided to resurface the floor of the sitting-room upstairs, by adding a complete layer of chipboard. It may sound a drastic decision, but we had niggled about it for months. Straining the bank balance by another £48 was just too bad. Don and Ray departed to purchase the wood and Ron continued the fiddly work of installing skirting board in the dining-room. I was, by this time, fully awake and decided to repair my mistake of the previous evening and give the upstairs windows a second undercoat, this time white.

It was a bright, if chilly morning, the Wednesday before Easter. The windows completed, I felt it was time for a change, a job that would make a spectacular improvement to the decor in the shortest possible time. With the ceilings awaiting their Artex, it seemed stupid to paint walls that would only get splashed later on. But the stairwell had an ordinary plastered ceiling so out came the white emulsion and I set to work. Disaster! I was using one of those five-litre cans of so-called 'budget emulsion' that many builders' merchants sell cheaply. There's no recognizable brand name, and as I applied the emulsion with my ancient, but still unrivalled lambswool roller I began to see why. I wish I had been told before beginning that new plaster is first best given a sealing coating of diluted emulsion. I simply sploshed a generous helping from the can into the tray and set to work. Either it coagulated into nasty white patches or it disappeared into the plaster leaving barely a trace. I persevered, not merely annoyed, but concerned at what the builders would think of my efforts. I considered myself to be a competent amateur do-it-yourselfer but the stairwell made me look like an inadequate know-all. But Don, Ray and Ron, to their credit, never commented. They were having their own problems. Ray returned with the chipboard in the lorry, only to find that each sheet was too large to negotiate the tight turn into the sitting-room at the top of the stairs. Thus each sheet had to be sawn in half before being transported upstairs.

On the second day Ray and Ron set to work on the ceilings, so that I might follow on with the walls. All the joints between the plaster-board first had to be taped (with what looked like sticky brown paper). Then came the Artex, which I was soon to discover is curious stuff. Once mixed with water it begins to harden almost immediately, which meant that Ray and Ron prepared only small batches at a time. Ron applied it to the ceiling rather in the manner of plaster, with Ray following behind with a special rubber-bristled brush to produce the stippled effect. Artex was splashed lavishly everywhere. I thought in my ignorant way that one could wipe off the splashes at one's leisure. Not so. The Artex, once set on the wrong places, had to be chipped off, inevitably leaving pock marks all over the plaster. Meanwhile I continued to wield the paintbrush. When we had rather casually decided to save about £200 off the builders' estimate by agreeing to do all the interior painting I know we had little idea of the scale of the undertaking. Acres and acres of bare plaster it

82

seemed to me: new woodwork that in most cases had been primed, but still needed successive treatments: sandpaper, undercoat, sandpaper again, possibly second undercoat, sandpaper and topcoat. I also realized that there were eight interior doors to be painted. Eight *new* doors, or sixteen sides. Being new meant that they first had to be primed, then came an undercoat and finally a topcoat.

Doing doors is a loathsome task at best, because you have to be on your guard all the time to ensure that the gloss coat doesn't run. I did one door on my third day with a three-quarter-inch brush, freehand, as it were. The idea of seven more, or fourteen sides, appalled me so much that I even toyed with the notion of paying the builders. Many weeks later, and the doors still unpainted, I mentioned the problem to an office colleague. 'Use a roller', he said. A roller? The master stroke, not only was the application of paint far more even, it also went on just thin enough to ensure it didn't run. Best of all it was much quicker, leaving more time for other things.

But to return to that Easter week: I did manage to complete the smaller of the two downstairs bedrooms, except for a gloss coat on the windows and the doors. Now all it needed was flooring on top of the basic concrete screed, curtains, and it would be complete. That third night I went to bed feeling greatly cheered. At least I had something dramatic to show for my graft, even if there were five more rooms to go. My sleeping arrangements were still unsatisfactory: it was bitterly cold. On Good Friday morning I woke up to snow. Suddenly I realized I had had enough. I packed my bags, took some photographs from my bedroom window of flakes actually falling over the Ouse, which was itself in full flood with the two side arches of the bridge almost completely submerged, and set off for London. The urge for civilization – and most of all for a bath – seemed irresistible.

At home Sue and I talked my ordeal through. Were we really taking on too much? I don't know what we might have decided if help hadn't been at hand – just when it was going to be most appreciated. Tony Askew, a friend and near neighbour in Highgate, volunteered with considerable enthusiasm to take a turn with the paintbrush. Tony meant what he said: his was no half-hearted

The view from our bedroom window, Good Friday morning.

gesture, but a full-bodied commitment. Weekend after weekend we headed north, sometimes for two days, sometimes just for one. We camped out several times, but in considerably less privation than I had put up with before, because Tony decided that there were certain priorities: getting the sitting-room fire alight for a start. Despite its minute grate I knew that our fire worked, because the builders had kept warm by it in the harsh mid-winter. Don cured its nasty propensity to go into reverse, as it were, by sticking a brick half-way up the chimney to improve the draught. Barely a wisp of ill-directed smoke have we suffered since. At first we relied on wood chippings and left-overs as fuel, later we bought curious reconstituted 'logs' from the Central Stores. But they burnt well.

Tony also believed in a congenial working atmosphere. Wine was considered essential, but not to an excess that impaired the quality of our work. Indeed I recall startling Sally Edwards from across Surrey Street at about nine o'clock one evening with a request for the loan of a corkscrew. It was dark, her husband was away on business, the children were in bed, and people in St Germans just didn't go

84

visiting that late in the evening. To accompany the wine and the rhythmic splish-splosh of the emulsion-charged roller on virgin plaster, he introduced me to the delights of the BBC World Service. Tony, being a high-up music studio manager at Broadcasting House, knew his wavelengths. But it took some readjusting to continue working while listening to an Edgar Wallace play – at three a.m., even if it was breakfast time in some former colonial territory.

Every weekend we used to wonder as we journeyed to St Germans just how much progress had been made by the builders in the intervening six days. But building work is not always spectacular. Nothing might appear to have been done, at least at first sight, and then one would open the bathroom door and suddenly find the bath, lavatory and washbasin in situ, where previously had been chaos. But we still had nothing more than a temporary electrical supply, and the plumbing remained unconnected. On May 12, that is some six weeks after Easter, Don was writing to say he was now awaiting a visit from the Water Board to approve the installation: only then would the mains be connected. Imagine our delight then, on Sunday May 25, when we arrived and Tony casually turned on a tap to find that it actually worked, and out flowed real water. There was much childish rivalry to be the first to test the bathroom facilities.

If I gave the impression that Tony and I did the decorating without assistance I malign Sue, Catherine (another of our Highgate neighbours) and the two Simons, ours and Tony's eleven-year-old son. Some weekends they invaded Bank Cottage like navvies, only taking time off for the occasional pint at the Crown and Anchor or sandwiches on the river bank. I only have to look back at our photograph albums to be reminded of progress inside: doing woodwork became tedious and the results were for the miniaturist to enthuse over. I soon realized that if I had been an artist only murals would have satisfied me; rooms changed spectacularly in the time it takes to roller on two coats of emulsion, or to paper the walls. Tony did the latter in the stairwell – and it glowed straight out of Habitat.

Outside, however, still looked like a building site, indeed, to be honest, I suppose that is what it was. I have endless pictures of

The hall freshly papered, but with the black tiles showing every footprint; Sue at work on the lobby.

various family and friends peering into trenches and holes in the back garden. Although, as previously related, the sewer had been laid, it seemed to me, as a layman, that it took ages to be connected to the house. One weekend a phallus-like plastic pipe protruded through the bathroom wall into the garden; the next it had been amputated, jointed and led, in apparently orderly fashion, into a drain. A week or two later the trenches had been filled in, and a small retaining wall, little more than eighteen inches high, was going up to keep the back garden at bay. But the bank, sloping as it did down to our path, remained an eyesore. I longed to see plants growing where grand specimens of rusting paint pot, rotten joist, empty tin can and the insidious torn polythene sheet still lay, entwined in the rapidly flourishing river bank grasses and desperately in need of grubbing out.

By the beginning of June, although Don was mildly rebuking me

86

for not yet completing the gloss coat on the dining-room woodwork, the flooring people arrived. Just as the painting of the walls had performed the transformation scene again and again for us as each room was completed, so the disappearance of the concrete under the vinyl repeated the magic, as if anew. The black vinyl tiles were first to go down, and almost immediately Sue regretted our choice. One only had to place a dusty foot on the shiny black surface to see that they were not going to be as practical as we thought. But the sheet vinyl in a mixed brown, yellow and caramel design on an off-white background, which we could afford only in the dining-room and kitchen, more than made up for our annoyance at the other. I don't wish to sound like a television advertisement, but it never shows the dirt, is warm to the bare foot, which the tiles certainly aren't, quite apart from being a joy to look at.

I digress. Being floored seemed to be the moment we had all been waiting for: fixing the date for moving in. It was hard to believe particularly when one thought back to three months before, polythene where the glazing should have been, no water, no sanitation, one naked light bulb and decoration hardly started. Work wasn't actually complete – we still had no porch, although the foundation had been cast – and a multitude of minor works remained: missing door fastenings, the fashioning of the fireplace surround, the connecting of the night-storage heaters, the fitting out of the kitchen, and the installation of the chimney flashing on the roof – nevertheless we decided on a date: Saturday June 28 1975.

With a deadline we went into overdrive, and so did the builders. I took the train from London two days before to see Don and take a combined look over the cottage; it seemed in good shape: the exterior woodwork had been painted, and only a few minor points had to be raised (even as we spoke the porch was going up), the most major being an old clay pantile on the Surrey Street frontage, which had become detached. All was now set for June 28.

CHAPTER NINE

In which

hot air threatens moving-in day,

fitted furniture fails to fit and

Sevenpence is sealed into his quarters

Moving-in day dawned in London with a cloudless sky. I was so excited I hardly slept the previous night. More than two years dreaming and, latterly, much hard work and over £4,000, had finally born fruit. Simon was staying next door with our neighbours, Maria with my parents. We hired a 35 cwt 'Luton' van, the ever-helpful Tony volunteered to share the driving and by eight a.m. we set off from Highgate – 108 miles to Bank Cottage, door to door.

The loading of the van had been achieved the night before. It seemed enormous, with storage space extending over the cab, but by the time we had finished there wasn't much left to spare. We had four beds, sofa, carpets, rush matting, blankets, linen, crockery, two tables, chairs, an old portable television, lamps and much other furniture besides, a store cupboard full of tins, a fridge, an electric stove and sundry smaller items. In fact, what one might expect when moving house, except that we had been storing this in London, initially in our flat and, since the death of Sue's mother, in hers too. As Sue pointed out, with feeling, not only were we making Bank Cottage habitable, but Highgate, too.

The journey north was not without incident. We had barely left Highgate, three of us on the bench seat, with Sevenpence, our middle-aged black labrador, making the best of it cramped at our feet, when Tony discovered that what we thought was ventilation was rapidly warming up into the heating system. Our attempts at switching it off failed, which was unfortunate, because the weather outside was rapidly meriting the phrase 'heatwave'. We opened the windows, but this didn't help Sevenpence, who was receiving the full blast at our feet; the only answer was to stuff the orifice with an old rag – this was the only time during the move that we regretted the balmy June weather. Our route to St Germans takes us up the A1, turning off for Huntingdon and thence along the straight roads of the fens (although unlike Roman roads they are interspersed with right-angle bends, which means rapid deceleration and changing down). Only a few weeks before with a laden car, but leaving early one Sunday morning Sue had done the 108 miles in one hour fifty-five minutes, an astonishing average. But on moving-in day we were forced to take it more slowly, although the 'Luton' van did have one compensation for me. At Stonea, a scattering of houses by the Sixteen Foot Drain, itself a fisherman's paradise in north Cambridgeshire, the road goes under the Ely-March railway line – at least cars go under, but the headroom is only seven feet. For vans such as ours there is a level crossing, with a bell to call the attention of the signalman in his box. In all my trips to Norfolk that spring I had never seen a train on the line, which as I am something of a railway enthusiast seemed like bad timing on someone's part. Imagine then my thrill when, as we pulled up at the crossing gate, a train could be seen approaching from the March, or north-westerly direction. As it was double-headed I announced that it must be a holiday special for Yarmouth which an inspection of the timetable later confirmed.

At Bank Cottage, brickwork for the porch had been completed since my visit on the Thursday and we began to unload. I suppose if we had been more methodical in our packing the last things in would have been carpets, so that at least these could have been unloaded first and laid, before we brought in the heavy furniture. But no: I have a photograph of the scene inside the front door. One word describes it – chaos. The trouble was that two of the fitted units for the kitchen failed to fit, by as little as three-eighths of an inch. Thus not only were we moving in, but Tony and I also had to do a rapid

conversion job on the Formica-topped corner unit before Sue could even begin on the kitchen. Tony showed his BBC skills to advantage by running new co-axial cable to the old television aerial (almost the only fitting to survive since we bought the cottage) and producing a better picture than we ever got on the same set in Highgate. After that everything seemed relatively simple: even cutting the rush matting to fit the sitting-room floor. I hardly expected the cottage walls to meet at perfect right angles, but I didn't expect such discrepancies, showing up most spectacularly downstairs on the vinyl flooring with its regular pattern being forced to disappear into the skirting board.

Looking around the cottage as I write makes me realize how fortunate we were in not having to rush into purchasing things in a hurry. By slowly accumulating in London we had the advantage of the classified advertisements in the *Hampstead and Highgate Express*. Indeed almost all our bedding came from households which were trying to recoup having just gone over to duvets. Crockery, a pine blanket box, even the electric stove were other classified booty. Sales, too, were a boon. It was my boast that I would never look at furniture unless it had a sale ticket on it. Thus the kitchen fittings, in particular, were of a quality far superior than we would otherwise have afforded, helped I must admit by mistaken labelling at John Lewis, who put their 'own brand' ticket (at sale price, too) on what would normally be the most expensive wall cabinets in the shop. But Sue's greatest triumph was an oddity: a two-gallon stone jar, inscribed 'Fryco Aerated Waters', which she saw in a north London junk shop, encrusted with grime and still clothed in its original basketware jacket. Once she got it home, the basketware fell away and a bath and a scrub in hot soapy water revealed its true identity. It now makes a magnificent floor lamp.

Once the van was empty and every item roughly in its place, we moved out onto the river bank for refreshment. It is at times like these that the river bank comes into its own: the Ouse is never without interest. Perhaps it was this weekend that we first identified the birds that darted around the bridge where their mud nests were

stuck to the underside of one of the arches. House-martins, said a
friendly passer-by as he walked his dog.

But our work was by no means complete. I hadn't realized just
how many items needed fixing to the walls. Gadgets by the handful
in the kitchen, wall-lights in the bedrooms; fittings in the bathroom – all had to be drilled and plugged in the masonry. I only
stopped when the Rawlplugs ran out. But I did have enough to put
up the curtain rails, an inexpensive adaptation of the old fashioned
rod and curtain-ring idea, but using dowel, unpolished wooden rings
bought by the dozen, and the largest hooks that our local hardware
store could sell us. For a start we put up curtains only in the
bedrooms, and a year later, as I write, we have progressed no
further, which, we have been surprised to discover, matters not a jot.
If you are a leap ahead of me and wondering about the bathroom, let
me say that it was one of our few extravagances: we had a blind made
to measure with a summery floral pattern that is bright enough to
cheer even the gloomiest winter day.

For Sue and Sevenpence this weekend was a true house-warming in that they slept in the cottage for the first time. Now Sevenpence usually spends the night on the vinyl floor in our kitchen in Highgate, but in offering similar quarters at the cottage we struck a problem. The door between the dining-room and the rest of the house had, as yet, no catch, and with no means of ensuring that it stayed closed it was a racing certainty that within five minutes of our retiring he would be padding up the stairs and scratching at our bedroom door to be let in. As the dining-room door opened inwards we couldn't simply prop a chair against it, unless we too wished to share Sevenpence's quarters for the night. In the end we sealed the door with Sellotape and prayed that it would hold – and it did.

Our return home was uneventful. The van, being several hundredweight lighter, fairly rattled down the A1, the level-crossing gates were open in our favour at Stonea, but hot air still seeped out into the cab, despite the rags. But we had achieved what we set out to do. We had taken up residence at Bank Cottage.

Mainly Play

CHAPTER TEN

In which
we learn what cottage living is all about

I did not hear the tile fly off our roof, but Sue found the dent in the car's bonnet next morning, the tile – still intact – alongside. We had arrived the previous afternoon, with the first of the autumn gales whipping across the Norfolk marshland. Standing on the river bank where six weeks before we had been soaking up the sun, we watched the tide rushing in and meeting the wind head on. Waves, white horses – it might have been a storm at sea.

The tile, an old clay pantile from the front, was the only casualty that night. We awoke to silence; the storm had blown itself out and the cottage seemed secure. We reassured ourselves that it had with-stood many a worse battering, for despite its exposed south-west position, the whole terrace had, after all, survived possibly two centuries.

The roof was one of the first parts of our cottage to be renovated when the builders began work. The existing clay pantiles were stripped off, with the unbroken ones retained so that when re-roofing began we could at least keep the front matching the rest of the terrace. But these old pantiles are a tiler's curse. Over the years – and ours might be half a century old, or more – they become brittle and tend to warp. Putting them back on a roof, which has had rotten timbers replaced and is now lined with roofing felt, is not a task the modern tiler welcomes.

Fortunately a tile off this roof is not quite the disaster it once would have been, as the roofing felt is waterproof, but as someone said next morning, we were lucky to suffer only a dent to the car; a foot one way and it would have gone through the windscreen. Even luckier it was not someone else's car. Indeed this autumn gale was to have a more severe sequel four months later in the New Year, but for the moment it served as a necessary corrective to our cottage euphoria brought on by the glorious summer weather which had us reaching for superlatives.

We had moved in the last weekend of June. Now Simon and Maria were longing to stay in Bank Cottage. Maria, nearly four and a half, had not been included in the painting parties of the spring. She studied each new set of photographs as we stuck them into the albums, but it wasn't the same: Maria wanted to see for herself. So the following Saturday we piled into the car and by noon we were unpacked and on the river bank. Maria was particularly excited by her bedroom with its bunk beds ('Can I sleep on the top, Mummy?') and the poster reproductions of Heath Robinson drawings on the walls. We explained to her, as we had to Simon, that the Great Ouse must be treated with great respect, even more so now as the long summer grass disguised the edge. Our local newspaper, the *Lynn News and Advertiser*, only the week before reported a child's death by drowning not far away upstream, but we soon discovered it was not the children, but our labrador who was the greater worry. Sevenpence kept running off and not returning until hours later, sopping wet, and muddy with it – presumably from the Ouse.

That first weekend we attended church, going to the family service and sitting in the pews carved with the St Germanus legend. In the Lady Chapel afterwards coffee and biscuits were served and we met the vicar, Cyril Rogers, and his wife. Everyone seemed so welcoming and friendly; certainly there was no disliking of 'furriners' here. Sally and Bob's daughter, Ann, was in the choir, but it came as a surprise to us to tot up numbers and discover that this choir was larger than the meagre congregation. Cyril Rogers turned out to be a man of many talents and interests: local historian, editor of the *Village News* (ecumenical, 2p an issue or 20p a year, and a circulation of several hundreds), and – perhaps the most winning ingredient as far as the children were concerned – he had a donkey in the vicarage garden. Indeed Bella's honking was a feature of village life when we arrived.

98

I thought at first it must be some eccentric steam whistle at Belmec, the small light engineering factory next to the garage and backing on to the vicarage, until I heard it one Sunday morning and asked out of curiosity if the work-force were on overtime.

Occasionally Cyril Rogers could be seen taking Bella for a walk through the village, even to see us one balmy day on the river bank, despite her dislike of water. But Bella was on her best behaviour – perhaps it was the fresh-cropped hay (the river authority having finally scythed the long grass on the bank) or the knowledge that she was pregnant (she gave birth to a Jack donkey the following May). It was Cyril Rogers who answered my queries about the history of the village. One mid-morning he brought round an envelope of local postcards, mainly photographs going back to the turn of the century. We were fascinated, not least because Bank Cottage figured in so many; the Great Ouse could be seen in all its

Postcard view of St. German's in the 1920s from the church tower. No flood banks protect the village and Bank Cottage (top right) from the Ouse.

moods – before the addition of flood banks, still bridged by a fragile looking wooden structure, even iced over in 1940. Someone else in the village was to tell us later that it was the sight of the icefloes that he remembered as much as the sound the river made that January, and also in the big freeze of 1947: it creaked and groaned with the movements of the tides under the ice. I borrowed the cards and had a selection copied; Sue had them framed, and today they decorate our dining-room.

That first weekend with the children was a trial run for the coming summer holidays. The cottage was, after all, primarily meant as a holiday retreat. We also had to ensure that everything was ready for our first visitors, the Askews, who were borrowing the cottage for a family holiday with their children (it seemed the least we could do; we owed Tony so much). We also detected the first hint of West Norfolk's unrivalled quality as a market garden. Every smallholding

100

appeared to sell strawberries by the roadside as well as vegetables, and particularly salad crops. We came home that first weekend laden.

As a result of the Askews' stay our knowledge of the area was considerably improved. Tony discovered a marvellous source of potatoes and onions at Magdalen, two miles up river. For tomatoes and cucumbers he recommended the Panks at Saddelbow, a village half-way between St Germans and Lynn. Sadly in the great storm the following New Year one of their glasshouses was totally destroyed. Sue bottled betroot, I pickled onions, and Tony started me home brewing. We soon realized the need for a deepfreeze to capitalize on the knockdown summer prices.

We rapidly came to appreciate the shop at the bottom of Surrey Street. There is hardly anything that the Central Stores hasn't got. On the food line it is as well stocked with basics as any supermarket, it also sells toys, seeds and other gardening requirements, clothes, shoes, haberdashery and even saved my standing in Simon's eyes, late one Saturday afternoon, when it produced the polystyrene glue he needed for model-making and which I had forgotten to purchase in Lynn. If I add that it is also licensed and seems to be closed but rarely, you will see that we are well blessed. The service from Peggy, Phyllis and Rose behind the counter is all that one could wish. No doubt if we lived on the other side of the river we would use the post office as our general stores and speak of it just as highly. But with the Central Stores so near who needs to go further afield?

The sun shone that first August day after day, only the farmers and the Anglian Water Authority worried about the lack of rain. We began by driving fifteen or twenty miles to one of the north Norfolk beaches, but we soon learnt that there was an admirable substitute for the sea, at least as far as swimming was concerned, in what is known locally as 'the cut'. This is the fourteen mile relief channel that runs roughly parallel to the Great Ouse from immediately south of King's Lynn to the sluice at Denver. At St Germans the two channels are about a quarter of a mile apart: the Ouse, wide, tidal, curving and at times exceedingly fast flowing; 'the cut' as wide, but straighter, freshwater and generally placid. It was dug after the 1947 floods as part of an elaborate preventative measure. Sensibly the river authority, recognising its recreational value, controls the coarse fishing (some of the best in England with coach-loads during the season coming from as far away as Sheffield and Leeds) and also a section reserved for water-skiing. Most people from St Germans swim just north of the water-skiing section. Simon, who could swim, but weakly at the beginning of the holidays improved several-fold by the beginning of September.

Bit by bit we began to assimilate West Norfolk. We were drawn into King's Lynn, not just because of the Georgian centre around Tuesday Market Place, but because of the market itself that once a week takes over. By eleven a.m. it is difficult to find parking space and it wasn't long before we cottoned on to a neat wheeze. We now drive to West Lynn, on the other side of the Ouse, park the car and take the ferry across to the quay that is barely two minutes from the market. Here you can buy almost anything, from clothes to vegeta-

Ferry across the Ouse at King's Lynn.

bles, double-glazing to carpet, ironmongery to antiques and much else besides. The children, Simon in particular, were enraptured from the start by one stall-holder whose staff of three are like a well-drilled vaudeville team. The star is John, a burly patter-merchant, with the gift of being able to sell almost everything he lays his hands on. His line is mainly blankets, linens, pots and pans, Japanese radios and bric-à-brac, but in the spring he unloaded Easter eggs, at Christmas it was mountains of boxes of chocolates. John is an entertainment in himself, even if one never buys anything he sells, although frequently one does. I gather he moves up and down the east coast markets, a different one each day. At Lynn he'll tease the mainly female crowd. 'I sold twelve dozen pairs at Wisbech last week. Don't you wear knickers here?' Blushes and laughter from the shoppers.

'While we're messing about,' he would go on, taking a quick drag from the inevitable cigarette, and wielding what Simon at first thought was a policeman's truncheon, 'let's clear these away. Now I've only got six of these. I'm going to offer them at one price and one price only.

'Now if you look up the High Street you'll find these continental bath sheets at £9 a pair.' In the background his two assistants, Joan and Malve, stretch what looks like a bath-towel, never mind bath *sheet*, to show its size.

'Look, if you and your old man get out of the bath together it will cover you both.' He pauses. The laughter rolls in, and he drags again at the cigarette. 'As I said: £9 in the shops. I won't ask you £8. I won't ask you £7. I won't even ask you £5. As I said these are going at one price and one price only.' Astutely he gauges the crowd, purses are being opened. If there are only six, no-one wants to get left out.

'Wait a minute. Hold your money ladies. I'm going even lower.' The audience presses closer. 'No I'm not going to ask you £5 or £4·50.' He bangs the truncheon hard on the wooden stall. 'The first six people to give me £4 – they're yours.'

Joan and Malve rush into action. Pound notes fly; large brown paper bags are produced. Miraculously John uncovers another pile

103

of the towels, and no one goes away disappointed. Next it's Swiss watches with a fancy ballpoint thrown in. 'Never seen daylight, Israelite or Fanny by bloody gaslight.'

Heaven knows where he gets the goods.

At the bottom end of the market Sue perueed the junk stalls. Not

long after we moved in to Bank Cottage she began a collection of old bottles and stoneware, preferably engraved with the product's name. Prices, compared with London, seemed ridiculously cheap, which is why, perhaps, our cottage is increasingly decorated with curios of the past such as a pair of flat-irons, the aforesaid bottles, a brass horn. Our other sources are the regular auctions, mainly of furniture, but also including almost anything you might expect to find inside a house, and many surprises besides. Where else would you pick up a vintage water softener that announces:

CHEAVIN'S 'SALUDOR' (SAFE WATER) FILTER
DRINKING WATER OF ABSOLUTE PURITY
BRITISH MADE THROUGHOUT
LEADLESS GLAZE

complete with original tap and spare filter?

It was in Tuesday Market that I first spotted Samphire. Samphire? This is the East Anglian name for Glasswort, *Salicornia europaea*, which Cumbrians know as Pickle Plant, Northumbrians as Semper while in Cheshire they call it Sampion. But by any name it is a delectable vegetable that grows on the salt marches and is very much a local delicacy. We consulted Richard Mabey's invaluable book, *Food for Free* *, and discovered that it should be cooked like asparagus. Our village was also visited by the samphire man. The

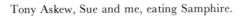

Tony Askew, Sue and me, eating Samphire.

* London, Collins, 1972

scene was timeless as he weighed out the samphire on old-fashioned brass scales.

Life in the village had a regularity, a solitude that appealed to us: it was a justification of the whole adventure. You can set your clock by the morning's postal delivery. In fact as I write Mrs Ramsbottom, a postwoman to St Germans for twenty-four years was to retire. Interviewed by the *Village News*, she recalled the occasional battles with the elements: wading through the 1953 floods and stepping over drowned piglets, being forced to forego her bicycle during one snow-bound Christmas and taking all day to deliver the mail on foot. According to Mrs Ramsbottom the quantity of mail has declined considerably, one lane alone in the past having nearly as much mail as the whole village does now, even though St Germans continues to grow. There has, she says, never been a time in her last three years when a home wasn't being built somewhere in the village. But telegrams come from Magdalen. We had one delivered during our first August by the sub-postmaster. His normal transport was out of commission and he had been forced, in order to deliver the telegram, to hitch a lift. But public transport, unlike in most country villages today, is not a problem in St Germans. Not only is there a bus service – privately run – but it makes a profit, running not merely on market day, but daily to suit workers and housewives. Daily that is except on Sunday: then, as the handwritten timetable in the post office notes, you have to walk.

St Germans is also unusual, I think, in having a small light engineering firm at its heart, invaluable in many ways, not least because it provides jobs that would otherwise have to be found four miles away in Lynn. I have mentioned Belmec before in connection with the vicar's donkey, but I suppose we first became conscious of it that first summer when as a change from its more mundane work the firm built a perfect, full-size replica of a steam chain engine exactly to the original specifications. Only the castings were made elsewhere. The chain engine was worked under its own steam into Lynn for an exhibition of the work of the great traction-engine builder, Frederick Savage. Such was the quality of Belmec's replica that the firm gained

106

a repeat order.

It was therefore, hardly surprising that Sue had considerable difficulty in persuading the children early in September that it was necessary to return to London in time for the autumn term. But we migrated to Norfolk at every possible occasion – weekends and half-term – and vowed to spend Christmas there as well. I don't know how we would have managed it, but for a friend who was travelling that way at the same time: he loaded his car with all our presents to each other, which otherwise would have had to have been left behind. It was the quietest Christmas we have ever known. On Christmas Day and even on Boxing Day we saw no one: St Germans battened down the hatches and seemed not to venture outside for the duration. We entertained ourselves with our presents and games. At the end of a delightful week we packed up regretting, as always, that we had to return to London. For once it was easy as Mumbo, our black cat, who accompanies us on every trip, was happiest staying indoors and, therefore, easily retrievable. But in the summer he only

107

appears for food and on one notorious occasion he was so content in the basement of the Old Hall's summer house that although it was time to go he simply would not appear. Ultimately Sue had to dangle a tin of cat food from a piece of string and slowly withdraw it, a kind of feline carrot-and-the-donkey enticement that Mumbo could not resist.

We left St Germans on December 27. The cottage was in fair order; we knew at last that planning permission had come through for the rendering, which was a relief as signs of penetrating damp were becoming obvious in our bedroom. The storage heaters were proving adequate, but we realized the need for an additional heater in the hall. In fact Bank Cottage seemed to be standing up to its first renovated winter remarkably well. That was until the following weekend. The first we knew of the severity of the gales that struck Norfolk was a call from Sally Edwards on the Saturday morning, January 3. Five of our old pantiles had been blown off, our television aerial hung drunkenly, held only by one bracket and the co-axial cable, part of a rear gutter had fallen and in the garden two panels of fence I had put up only three months before had keeled over. But our damage was slight compared to Bob and Sally's cottage.

As Sally remarked a few days later: 'I have never been so frightened in all my life.' Nor was she dramatizing the gales that had gusted to 105 m.p.h. over north Norfolk. The north-west wind blew up suddenly. Being on the east bank of the Ouse our two cottages took the full force, and, inevitably, something had to give: but when hefty pantiles are picked up by the wind and flung around like so much featherdown anything that gets in the way is certain to be damaged. Thus it was with Sally and Bob's cottage. Windows were shattered in their lean-to porch. There were moments when they thought the wind, now that it was swirling savagely around inside as well as out, would lift the porch roof right off. All attempts at barricading the gaping windows with boxes proved hopeless. The wind merely sucked them into the maelstrom outside.

Their car was parked in Surrey Street between our houses. Bob decided that it ought to be moved to the lee of the house, but his problem was how to safeguard against decapitation from the flying tiles outside. Finally he emerged, helmeted in a bucket, only to find that his car had already suffered a pounding: the bonnet dented and scratched by the flying tiles. Further inspection outside showed that their garden gates, large and seemingly indestructible, had been torn from their substantial posts. Upstairs the floor of one of the children's bedrooms was visibly quivering. Finally at about one in the morning the wind appeared to subside, although it was to give several cathartic gusts during the night.

News of the gale began to circulate. Trees were down everywhere, and all the roads into King's Lynn were blocked. Farmers with glasshouses had suffered appalling damage, but help was readily at hand as it always seems to be in our part of Norfolk. Our television aerial was made safe; Don Noyce took a look at the roof and confirmed that it was watertight despite the missing tiles.

I visited St Germans the following Thursday to check that all was well. Gale stories were to be heard on all sides. The *Lynn News and Advertiser* used the words 'Devastation and Chaos' to describe Snettisham beach on the east side of the Wash near Sandringham. The remains of caravans and chalets were everywhere. But inventiveness, as always seems the case in times like these, was to the fore. Struggling to prevent a bungalow roof from being torn away, two couples secured it with ropes, not just to the ground, but to a Land-Rover for extra weight. Roof and car were both intact next morning.

Many months later I was telling the story to Ray Noyce, who lives ten miles to the south of us at Southery. He had awoken that Saturday morning to find his neighbour's hut was scattered all over a nearby field. He went next door, thinking that he ought to pass on the information, only to find that his neighbour was all too aware of the hut's fate. The previous night, seeing that it was being battered alarmingly by the gale he went outside into the garden and tied down the roof with the only suitable material to hand – the garden hose. Then before his eyes the wind made a supreme effort, the hut rose, pulling against the hose, finally stretching it until it snapped.

109

CHAPTER ELEVEN

In which

we harvest our first crop . . . of builder's rubbish;

our garden's future is decided;

rendering finally takes place; and

we import beans from Somerset

I gave up counting after one hundred, but still the pile grew. Digging over ground last occupied by builders is like fishing in a murky canal and bringing up nothing but old boots or straining your line past breaking point on some rotten under-water hulk. In Bank Cottage garden the catch was bricks, discarded timber, crumpled paint posts, yards of tangled, rusting wire, in fact the detritus of years of neglect followed by eighteen months of renovation and modernization. It was not surprising that the shaft of my spade snapped as I tried to shift what turned out to be a substantial part of the old septic tank.

Our back garden is a small squarish plot and, like the house, it runs parallel to the river. Originally I had thought of it as a patio, with perhaps a handkerchief of grass to sit out on. With chest-high, mellowed red brick walls to north and west as well as the bonus of the Old Hall's summer-house in one corner and a toolshed (formerly the outside lavatory) in the other it seemed ideal. But it was our experience the summer we moved in that for sitting out there was nothing to beat the river alongside. Thus this first summer we left the plot to the groundsel, shepherd's purse, deadly nightshade and other annual weeds, at the same time giving thanks that it was host to

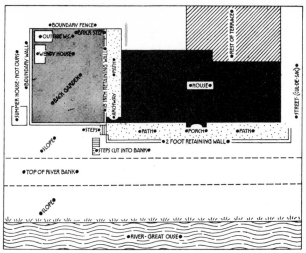

nothing so insidious as ground elder or bindweed. As to its future subconsciously we let it percolate. Horticulturally-minded friends were quick to approve: 'never rush the planning' being a grand gardening maxim. But I did put up a fence on the party wall to the east, only to suffer the ignominy of part of it succumbing to the first winter gale.

It was a perfect summer followed by a dry autumn and with near drought conditions vegetable prices soared, headed by potatoes. By Christmas they had gone into orbit. Perhaps this was what finally made up my mind, and Sue certainly did not disagree: we would turn over the back garden to vegetables. The first digging took place in Christmas week with a searing north-easterly fresh off the North Sea to encourage one to keep labouring, if only for warmth. I also began planting: on the river side of the west garden wall I envisaged raspberries and loganberries. Digging over their permanent homes I brought up an unbroken bowl of a clay pipe. This was the first such find for the best part of a year. During early excavations Don Noyce unearthed several pipe bowls and broken stems, ranging in age across two centuries. Thus Sue's interest in the archaeology of Bank Cottage had burgeoned, particularly as the builders were to turn up many more pipe bowls and broken stems. But the surprise discovery

111

of an unbroken bowl brought her to the scene with more delicate tools than my garden spade. But although she scratched through the soil, and particularly the sticky yellow clay that had been disturbed during excavation for the extension, she went unrewarded.

Meanwhile Maria became perturbed when I began digging in the back garden. Here was the magnificient Wendy House, built originally for Bob and Sally's children next door and now handed down to her on loan. Would it have to go? I reassured her and after re-siting it to face south to catch the sun, partially hide the tool-shed and enable her to communicate with Sue through the open kitchen window, she set to work and turned it into her version of our village shop, the Central Stores.

We could turn over the back garden to vegetables because we also have a slender patch at the front, as well as the river bank, or at least the part that slopes towards Bank Cottage. Here would be our flower garden, even if it had changed somewhat since the original April day when I had first seen the property three years before. Don Noyce, our architect, realized from the beginning that to inject the essential damp course into the walls of the cottage would mean lowering the path that ran between it and the river bank. In the end he reckoned that three feet would be sufficient, but that was by no means all, something would also have to be done to prevent a river bank landslide. As a by-law-abiding architect he consulted the Great Ouse River Authority. They sent along their District Engineer, who suggested a small retaining wall. Fortunately he was also a gardener. The bank, once stabilised, could be regrassed, he said, planted with bulbs and generally cultivated. Indeed, this is what we have done, although not exactly to his specification.

We have some thirty feet of bank, but it is only three feet wide and rising about three feet from the retaining wall at an angle of, on average, forty-five degrees. During the first summer holidays in residence we only cut the wild grasses, marvelled at the self-sown but enormous poppies, and nurtured half a dozen nasturtiums from seed put in by Simon. By the end of the summer I had planted for the future putting in more than one hundred mixed daffodils and two

112

score tulips in the hope that they would provide us with one spring's magnificent display. This, they did, coinciding precisely with our arrival for Easter the following year.

I had first brooded on the Bank Cottage gardens the winter the builders were in residence. My method, making scale drawings and filling them with copious planting schemes, had been a diverting experience for several evenings and led eventually to a master plan and my placing an extensive order with a Surrey nursery for delivery the following spring. My eagerness had leapt ahead of the actual time scale and I was therefore left with no alternative but to find temporary quarters for them in our London garden. Our eventual decision to lay emphasis on vegetables meant that some purchases had to be allotted new homes. But otherwise the master plan remained, at least in theory. I realized – or at least dredged the information from some horticultural recess in my mind – that to dig out the grasses from the bank would destroy the network of roots that kept the soil together and stopped it tumbling onto the path below. Otherwise I would merely be undoing in one summer just what the river authority's engineer was trying to avoid when he recommended a retaining wall. As a result of this line of thought I dosed the grasses with a paraquat week-killer and only disturbed the soil when digging individual holes for plants. First, at strategic intervals along the bank, I put in three low-growing and spreading roses – Wichuriana, Max Graf and Paulii – with the idea that they would eventually combine ground cover with colour. Elsewhere I made homes for potentillas, spiraea, and mallow grown on from cuttings taken on a disused railway-line embankment in London. With planting under way, the builders delivered the scaffolding in order to render the exterior walls. It would, Don politely informed me, be pointless to continue when cement would shower the ground like snow. But before the little plant life remaining in the putative front garden was decimated under this onslaught, I rescued several self-sown columbines and perennial sweet pea seedlings.

The actual rendering took place during Easter week, or four months after planning permission had finally been granted. (It was judged too risky to begin any earlier, the winter frosts being sudden and vicious, spelling doom to newly applied cement.) The weather the first day and a half was perfect. First on went the waterproof coat which Ron, the plasterer (only the materials in rendering differ, not the technique) later scored with a makeshift comb to provide a key for the second and smooth finish. After lunch on the second day he applied the second coat to the river frontage and left for home. By tea-time it was drizzling, by seven a solid night's rain was upon us. Farmers were jubilant, but my cheers were muted as I saw what it was doing to that afternoon's labours. The newly-applied, and still soft cement was severely pock-marked. It looked like a sandy beach after a thunderstorm. Worse was to follow. Near the lantern on the south-west corner two dollops of cement fell away leaving patches that looked astonishingly like Mercator's projection of Australia, and more tenuously, New Zealand. It rained solidly for twenty-four

114

Ron applies the first coat of the cement render.

Combing the first layer in readiness for the top coat (right).

hours and it was not until the day following that our building team returned. Ron swore a bit, called for soft sand and was soon applying a further, but finer coating of cement to the damaged wall. Australia and New Zealand were soon to disappear.

The rendering completed meant that we were at last eligible for the second half of our improvement grant, a most welcome cheque for £500. A month later, at the Spring Bank Holiday an impressive-looking letter arrived from West Norfolk District Council:

Housing Act, 1957
Order determining Closing Order in lieu of Demolition Order in respect of a House

In layman's language the closing order put on the cottage three years before had finally been lifted. Considering that we had been living in the cottage for nearly a year it was about time too.

Once the builders removed their scaffolding I returned to the garden. Friendly plantsmen had been quick to offer gifts. Jan Stephens, the botanically-minded arts sub-editor at *The Times*, brought me some euphorbia lathyrus. Additionally I put in chrysanthemum maximum, hypericum and heuchera grown from seed in London, as well as rooted tufts of a mossy saxifrage. The children added their contribution: nasturtium again and a sprinkling of annuals.

When we had first seen Bank Cottage a yellow climbing rose of name unknown scaled the river-facing wall, a pure white perennial sweet pea seemed to sprout from the brickwork, an indication of how damp the walls were, and a mound of arabis decorated the coal house door. This planting was so successful that recreating the formula seemed the best basis on which to build.

The ground level around the house having been reduced during the renovations, it did not take me more than a spade or two's research to discover that the soil was a mixture of yellow clay and sand (just like our part of north London). Just to keep me on my toes I kept stabbing broken bricks and stones, hardly the best foundation for any plant. Digging the hole for one rose I encountered a strip of yellow polythene. Thinking it was more builders' rubbish I pulled. Instead of easing out of the clay it stretched, eventually snapping. I tried again. Only then did Simon standing by, start reading the words on the polythene scraps: BEWARE! LIVE CABLE. I had dug down to the cottage's electrical supply.

The end gable of our west wall fronting onto the river rises twenty feet and more from the ground. Originally it did not have windows, but we decided that the view across the Ouse was too good to miss, quite apart from the need for light. Thus two new window frames were incorporated upstairs, but there is still a considerable expanse of wall, an ideal site for one of those great climbing roses that think nothing of scaling twenty feet. I consulted books, catalogues and experts and finally decided on Longicuspis, because it flowers in late July and August, just the time when all the family are in residence. In fact, if there has been one credo behind the garden planning it is to emphasize the mid- and later-summer flowering plants. At the front of the cottage, on the corner, I put in another powerful climber,

Newly planted roses with the path freshly gravelled.

Gloire de Dijon and against the summer house at the bottom of the back garden another called Alister Stella Grey for its buttonhole buds of yellow, which, I thought, would show up well against the burnt red of the old brickwork. But it never took hold and died in the 1976 drought. Elsewhere against the house I put in clematis, the variety Jackmanii Superba because it has served me magnificently in London.

Our porch seemed to me to be particularly important. Although it was not the original, much to Sue's disappointment, we have been exceedingly glad of it, particularly in the winter when it offers just that modicum of shelter to the front door. Ideally, it should, I suppose, have an outer door, but this was one expense we postponed to the future. I felt that the porch should have plants growing up, over and around it, and that in true cottage fashion, they should be plants with plenty of scent. I plumped for honeysuckle and jasmine. One of the inspired touches of Don Noyce's plans for Bank Cottage was the incorporation of an arch linking the garden wall with the extension. I wondered at first if it should be the frame for a wisteria, but decided in the end that another honeysuckle, but of a different variety, would be better.

When I completed the digging of the back garden there had been little rain (as Ron remarked as he was doing the rendering: 'February filldyke missed out this year') and we were already being commanded to ration our needs. The Anglian Water Authority appeal included what was to become a memorable tip: 'Don't flush the lavatory as often as you would normally. If you place a clean brick in the cistern one and a half pints of water can be saved at every flush.' We were later to learn that if every household in the land did likewise Britain's 1976 water problems would be no more. Certainly East Anglia was drier than I had ever previously seen it. Brush fires were common, the dykes and drains were perilously low; even as early as that Easter there were parts of our back garden where the soil was dry a spit deep in some places. By July we were praying for nightly downpours. With our irregular visits during May and June, the river bank in particular had dried out, many of our poor plants,

120

with only a few months' footing in the soil, being unable to survive. I lost uncounted herbaceous perennials, two of my precious climbing roses, several spiraea and some of the mallow, although in the vegetable garden the tomatoes and courgettes showed little sign of dehydration.

These had gone in over Whitsun. Previously I had opted for basic summer and autumn crops. I put in the best part of a stone of potatoes, although that spring seed prices reflected the current economic necessity to grow one's own: in Tuesday Market in King's Lynn, a five pound bag of another variety, Arran Pilot, was fetching 40p, and none too promising specimens either. In addition we sowed dwarf French beans, lettuces and radishes. For the future we started a seed-bed with cauliflower and savoy cabbages. There was one other vegetable, a curiosity; describing it is how I shall finish this chapter.

Just before leaving London that Easter, one of my reviewers on *The Times*, the novelist Tim Heald, offered me a packet of Martock beans 'as grown in the ancient parish since the thirteenth century'. Later I reported in *The Times* that the beans looked like 'wrinkled black marbles', that they were a strain peculiar to Somerset and that they came complete with the legend on the packet: 'If you do shake a Martock man you do hear the beans rattle'. We treated the beans as something of a joke: if they blossomed and gave us a meal or two so much the better; if not it didn't matter. They were an eccentricity with which to garnish our uncommon, but intriguing plot.

That would have been that, but my article found its way into the hands of Ralph Whitlock, the Wessex writer who contributes a marvellous, discursive and richly informative countryside column to the *Western Gazette*, the local newspaper for Somerset and east Devon. Whitlock knew Martock, but not its beans, so he investigated, reporting as follows:

My first emissary went into a store in Martock and enquired innocently: did they know what Martock beans were, and where could a friend get a packet? They just fell about laughing, she told me. 'We be Martock be-ans', they said. 'All Martock folk born

121

and bred be Martock be-ans.'

Another friend of Whitlock's, living in Martock, added further information:

In the old days Martock men had a great reputation for hard drinking. Their capacity was said to be even greater than that of the men of Middlezoy, which is saying a lot. At harvest-time, every morning when the harvesters went out with their reaphooks to cut the corn they were given a two-gallon cask of cider . . . They were also given five handfuls of black beans, which they put inside their shirts. Their belts, of course, prevented the beans from slipping down and falling out of their trouser legs.

Well the purpose of the beans was to keep the harvesters sober enough to stand on their feet. As they got through those two gallons of cider they would, between swigs, eat handfuls of beans, which counteracted, to some extent, the effects of the drink. So now you can see why, if you shake a Martock man you do hear the beans rattle.

The beans were obviously field beans, or tic beans. In the old days farmers would keep their own seed and use it for year after year, generation after generation, century after century. There may well be beans on farms around Martock that have grown them for hundreds of years, long enough to have become a special strain.

We had obviously started something. Tim Heald looked back in his files. He had mentioned Martock and its beans in an article about the West of England in the *Radio Times* and had received several letters, including one in dialect:

'Tis like this yer. The varmers roun yer use to gro be-ans to veed the hosses, the raison be tha we got good grou roun yer an thas wat be-ans da like. Mine you they be a tricky crop to gro and thas why mose varmers have ge-id em hup. The honely time you da yet anythink bout Mardick be-ans now-a-days is wen they da call our vootball te-am the Mardick Be-ans.

122

Another correspondent included a splendid, if quaint poem entitled
'Martock Peas and Beans' written 150 years ago by the parish
church organist, a Mr Pomeroy. The relevant verse runs:

> For if a Martock man you take
> In anger, some will tell ye
> The peas, and beans a noise will make
> By rattling in his belly.
> But where's the man, say if you can,
> That is so rash to do it
> As dares to tan a Martock man;
> He'll soon find cause to rue it.

But the final authoritative word came from the Vicar of Martock,
the Reverend Peter Coney. He confirmed what we knew, adding that
'they have been growing on at least one farm for time out of mind.
The earliest reference to them is in the manorial account rolls of
1293-4. I obtained a supply from the farmer and normally part with
them in return for donations to the church restoration fund.'

I doubt that the export of Martock beans to Norfolk will ever
become a major traffic. Our first crop was reasonable in quantity
and promptly installed in the freezer, having first been podded by
Maria one morning on the river bank. No doubt in a wetter summer
the crop would have been heavier. But I am pleased to think that
Bank Cottage garden has contributed a footnote, if nothing more to
West Country horticultural history.

CHAPTER TWELVE

In which
the Great Ouse stakes its claim,
floods abound and are prevented,
the wild life (and death) make an impression, and
a boat appears once again
on the river bank

Our river, the Great Ouse, has kept cropping up in this narrative. If, subconsciously, it was the reason we bought Bank Cottage, then it deserves a chapter to itself. The river is the miracle ingredient, the added attraction that makes our cottage more than just a country retreat from the pressures of London. It is a magnet, a source of fascination during even the shortest of stays. Sue says now how lucky we were to find it. Certainly it is hard to imagine us owning a cottage anywhere else other than by a river, this river, unless it was near the sea – and that would be farther away from London.

Until the 1950s it was possible to walk out of Bank Cottage's porch, cross a path, and come immediately upon the river – perhaps twenty feet from house to water. But the floods of 1947 and 1953 were two high-water marks that could not be ignored as the marsh and fenlands south of the Wash were decimated, as was much of the East Anglian coastline. In those days it only needed high spring tides, combined with northerly gales, to force more and more water up the rivers where they met the already swollen fresh water flowing off the land. Disaster was assured. In 1947 a deep frost meant that the land could absorb little of the water. Thousands upon thousands of acres were submerged, the drainage channels proving inadequate, as had long been known, although just how bad could only now be seen. In 1953 the curving Ouse broke in a number of places near St Germans. Immediately opposite us on the other bank is a barn, one end of which looks newer, testimony that it succumbed to the flood's wrath. Nor was our side immune. Our good friend Hubert Gorbould, who owns nearby gravel pits and much else besides, recalls Surrey Street awash and the downstairs rooms of cottages flooded.

I knew none of this when we decided to buy Bank Cottage. What I saw was six-foot high flood banks that are flat on top and wider than a Cornish double-hedge. Thanks to Downham Rural Council's Mr Hurst we have our sitting-room upstairs which means that we do, as he forecast, get a marvellous view over the river and magnificent sunsets. The flood bank has certainly been our protection. If we had been living in St Germans in the Middle Ages we could have expected serious flooding at least once every decade. We would also have been required to contribute substantially to the maintenance of the Ouse embankments. But in 1973 ignorance was, indeed, bliss. Flooding? I didn't need to inquire, as the Borough of King's Lynn, before granting our mortgage had consulted their insurers. Records were consulted and the verdict pronounced: there would be no additional premium as they were satisfied there hadn't been any flood damage since 1953.

Three years later and even we wondered. On the fourth day of 1976 the old combination of spring tides coupled with northerly

Fifty years separate these two views of the riverbank.

gales caused the river authority to declare a Red Alert, the ultimate in warnings. The Trewins in Highgate were unaware of this, but Tony Askew, to whom we lent the cottage that weekend, reported that the river rose one foot higher than ever previously recorded. But the flood bank proved its worth: the water leaving a freeboard of four feet on our side.

Living in St Germans we began to learn about our flat, but never tedious landscape. 'The big sky' as one friend put it perfectly. This is the Marshland, I was told. Marshland? In my ignorance I had thought that all land between Cambridge and the Wash was known as the Fens, but I was quickly corrected. The peatlands between Peterborough, Ely and Brandon are Fens, once flooded in winter by fresh water, while to be precise one should describe the silt soil nearer the Wash and bounded by King's Lynn and Wisbech as the Marshlands, salt water being the main enemy here. Thus the depredations of the Middle Ages.

By the early seventeenth century landowners began to search for ways to drain the peat and keep out the sea. Vermuyden, the great Dutch engineer, produced detailed schemes, many of which were adopted piecemeal, but whose grand design for the Ouse had to wait three hundred years. Successive engineers studied the problem and produced broadly the same answer: that relief and cut-off channels were necessary to the east of the river, that is on our side. Norwich City Library has a map, dated 1724, that shows a 'cutt propos'd of 200 or 250 foot wide' from a quarter of a mile north of our cottage to King's Lynn, with the Ouse snaking its roundabout way to the Wash. But something more considerable was necessary. In 1940 an eleven-mile relief channel was announced from Denver Sluice to St Germans. The war intervened and the 1947 floods showed the inadequacies of even this scheme, so the cut was extended to just south of King's Lynn, making fourteen miles in all, and begun in 1954. As I have previously pointed out it is known in St Germans as 'The Cut'. In fact it took ten years to complete, a massive digging operation across rich farm land with many new concrete bridges and roads realigned. The cost: £10,425,000. Whereas St Germans was

The Jenyns Arms
DENVER SLUICE

GREAT OUSE RIVER BOARD
DENVER SLUICE BRIDGE

Tolls Authorised to be taken every time of
 passing this bridge and Sluice   s.d.

For every person passing on foot on Easter Monday. 1.
For every Horse, Mare, Gelding, Mule or Ass. 1.
For every Ox, Cow, or Large Cattle.   1.
For every Sheep, Lamb, Pig, or Calf.   1.
For every Cycle, 3 or less number of wheels.   1.
For every Cart or Carriage with two wheels
 including one horse, Mare, Gelding Mule or Ass
 if drawn by same.   } 6.
For every Horse, Mare, Gelding Mule or Ass in addition. 1.
For every Waggon, Road Trolley, Van or Motor Cycle
Implement, Thrashing or other Machinery
Vehicle or carriage with four wheels if not laden. } 1.0.
For the like if laden.   2.0.
For every Thrashing or Traction Engine or Steam
 roller whose full load weight does not exceed 5 tons 2.6.
N.B. Traction Engines or Steam rollers whose full
 load weight exceed 5 tons are prohibited from
 going over this Bridge and Sluice.

EXEMPTIONS

Members of the Board and Officers, Servants and
workmen of the Board when engaged on the business
of the Board.
The Inhabitants on the west side of the sluice when
 going or returning from diveine Service on Sunday

THIS TOLL DISCONTINUED APRIL 1963

neatly sandwiched, with the river and the relief channel three-quarters of a mile or more apart, another Wiggenhall, St Peters, was blighted. Once it was on the road to Watlington, a village on the other side of the railway, but there was a limit to the number of bridges thought necessary across the new channel and St Peters ended up as a cul-de-sac. It was a final blow. In the late 1920s, its magnificent medieval church was declared unsafe and lost its roof. Hugging the east side of the Ouse, with the flood bank built into the tower, it stands today open to the elements, but still cared for locally, and still the scene of an annual service on its saint's day. When I first met our vicar he was greatly concerned at the state of St Peters, but he despaired that money would ever be forthcoming to save it from complete collapse. But in April 1976 came the good news that the diocese authorized the repair and consolidation of the St Peters fabric 'sufficiently to contain and arrest the current deterioration . . . and to preserve the building as a ruin'.

St Peters Church is a mile upstream from St Germans, a splendid walk where one hot August day Maria and Simon, with Edward, a boy from Highgate, found more than thirty different wild flowers in bloom. The river curves gently, at most tides disguising the treacherous sandbanks. When the Ouse was a main artery of trade, craft needed pilots. Dorothy Summers, in her book about the river* recounts that gangs of lighters needed guidance up river from Lynn, through St Germans to Magdalen Bridge, but downstream pilotage usually began at St Germans bridge. Four horses, three men and two boys were considered the essential minimum, with wages totalling about 18s a day. Dorothy Summers quotes an account by a waterman of a particularly difficult passage:

> Going down from German's with a loaded Gang with Corn, in a hard Gale of Wind, I expected to lose our Lives, Gang and all, and went on Shore, near the Ball Fleet; Five Lighters filled full of water, One Lighter had none in her, and one about Fifteen Comb of wet Corn – those which filled with Water were loaded with Barley, Wheat and Rye – the Wheat was safe, the Barley and Rye wetted.

* *The Great Ouse: the History of a River Navigation.* Newton Abbot, David and Charles, 1973

The ruined St. Peter's church.

But at least traffic could get through. Early in the fourteenth century, the river had been terrorized by Robert Montalt, Lord of the Manor of Rising who camped with his supporters by St Germans Bridge. He is said to have demanded tolls not only from the river traffic, but road travellers, too. Could he, perhaps, have established himself precisely where Bank Cottage now stands? St Germans Bridge was the first crossing place on the Ouse, King's Lynn having to make do with ferries. No wonder then that the village, as a base for pilots and a necessary funnel for cross-country trade, thrived and at one time supported five public houses.

The Ouse today is flowing faster thanks to man's channelling of its sources, but this has at least one disadvantage. The swiftness of flow means that the river bottom is scoured and the silt disturbed, thereby invariably clouding the water. Simon went in one evening at high tide with Alan Edwards, and they emerged afterwards covered in a rime of silt. But the Ouse is a beachcomber's paradise: one day at an unusually low tide, Alan, Simon and Christopher, a boy from across the river, donned boots and trawled an impressive catch: old bottles to add to Sue's collection, a stainless steel kitchen knife, and an old carpet beater. But a more traditional catch is the eel, and local fishermen also go for a plaice-like flat fish by dragging a barbed metal bar along the river bottom from behind a boat. At first we were told that these were unfit for eating, their taste reflecting too pungently the muddiness of the Ouse. But during our second summer we learnt differently.

One Tuesday morning, just before we were leaving for market, a fourteen-foot clinker-built open boat powered by an outboard hove into view from Lynn on a slow zig-zag path. Here was, it turned out, a man and his son, dragging for fish, even an occasional plaice. They tied up below our cottage and Sue offered the man tea. In fact he was going to the Crown and Anchor for a drink, but he handed Sue two of the fish and refused any payment. We gave one to Sally and put ours into water. Returning from Tuesday Market we found the fish stiff – *rigor mortis*? Not knowing what to do next Sue took it down Surrey Street to the Howmans who live on the corner. Mrs Howman

131

was delighted to show Sue how to gut the fish, which she called a 'butt'. That evening, and rather gingerly, Sue and I had it for supper. Our verdict: meaty if a mite bland.

Our fisherman explained that the flat fish feed on the bottom of the river swimming against the tide. To catch them the boat flows with the tide dragging her lethal looking metal bar. The hooks catch the fish which tries to escape by swimming hard forward, only impaling itself still firmer onto the hook. Catches vary, but this fisherman said he had once taken two hundredweight between Lynn and St Germans. Next day he brought us half a dozen more, which were gutted and placed in the freezer.

To the non-participant the Ouse offers other attractions. The bird life is exceptional: a pair of herons nests a mile down river, geese of many varieties regularly fly over, and frequently we are visited by swans (once as many as a dozen, but more frequently individually or in pairs). They will usually respond to stale bread cast upon the water, and on one memorable occasion Sue enticed a swan up the sticky mud at low tide so that it was almost eating out of her hand. The Ouse is the only place I have ever seen a swan getting airborne. The effort was considerable, the length of runway prodigious. The swan might well have been a jumbo jet. I wondered if it was injured, but a local enthusiast was to tell me that all swans are like this. Indeed a swan is a prisoner without a long stretch of water, he said,

as it cannot take off from land. But the greatest attraction, possibly because they are seen less frequently, are the seals from the Wash, which usually appear to coast in on the flood-tide. Baby seals have even been marooned on the bankside below our cottage.

Nicer by far than the sight that greeted us on the first day of our first summer holiday at Bank Cottage. Coming down stream twenty feet apart were what looked like two enormous hummocks of earth, but as the first came under the bridge a shout went up: 'It's a cow – and dead, too.' Indeed so was the second. We debated how they might have died: did they fall in and drown? Were they found dead and the carcasses dumped? Suddenly swimming in the Ouse seemed less of an attraction. Their passing by reminded me that earlier in the summer, just as we were leaving one Sunday afternoon after a day's painting, we were surprised by a bullock looking down on us from the top of the flood bank. Presumably it came from the grazing land just down river from Bank Cottage. A fence, with a stile, is usually a sufficient barrier, but such was the lowness of the tide that the bullock had been able to paddle round to our side. We drove off leaving someone else to raise the farmer.

We watched the carcasses disappear around Eau Brink bend towards King's Lynn and the Wash. Much later that day we were again on the bank with the tide now flooding in. Sue was, I know, hoping for seals and had the binoculars trained down river. Suddenly and with disbelief in her voice, she cried out: 'It's those dead cows again.' Sure enough the carcasses, possibly a little lower in the water, were coming in on the tide. They soon passed by on their way up river. We cogitated: possibly the fourteen miles of tidal Ouse precisely matched the speed of the tide, otherwise surely these carcasses would have disappeared into the Wash, never to return? With the tide flooding for six hours, that meant an average speed, if my mathematics were correct, of just over two miles an hour. Next day the carcasses were farther apart, and one was now almost under water; a day later we were left with only one and after that we never saw it again. We worked out that it must have travelled past us at least twelve times and covered more than 160 miles.

Not long after we arrived an 'eagar' was forecast. We asked for elucidation and were told that 'eagar' is the local name for bore, as in Severn bore. They occur as low tides are on the turn; the sea rushes in, creating a wall of water which pushes all before it in a deceptively leisurely wave. We imagined something several feet high and were disappointed when in trickled a wave barely twelve to eighteen inches high. If it occurs at weekends a plethora of small craft wait at Lynn and then cash in on its swell in assisting them up river. It was on one such occasion that a woman looking over the bridge suddenly exclaimed: 'Oh! I see. I wondered why the boat's wash was so far in front, rather than behind.'

Early in September just before the holidays came to an end, Bob Edwards bought a boat, clinker-built, with an outboard engine. With his children he collected it in Lynn and chugged up river to St Germans on the tide, a journey that took longer than we all expected, so much so that it was twilight as he hove into view. We helped Bob haul it onto the bank. It had been patched on the bottom and would need some work if a leak was to be cured. But a boat on the bank was a sign of the resurgence of this small corner of our village. A year later two others were intermittently parked there. Once the Ouse had thronged with craft, as Dorothy Summers has recorded: usually transport, coal, building materials and wine up river, returning with agricultural produce – mainly corn and malt. The trade has gone, only pleasure craft use the waterways today, including the occasional water-skier. It is a long way from Arthur Ransome and Kenneth Grahame. But one of Cyril Rogers' poscards shows several boats tied up at a rickety-looking jetty by the Crown and Anchor, just upstream from us. The coming of the flood bank changed all that. But not for good, surely?

Postscript

Postscript

In which
we are treated to the excesses of fire and water

We had been buying maggots at Colin Stevens' fishing shop in Lynn. The white round plastic container looked like something you might use for storage in the fridge, but less obviously for its contents. Take off the ventilated lid and inside was a mass of squirming life, in rather basic form, all ready for the fisherman's line. Simon had yet to try out his rod, but the gear looked impressive. He had earned some money from *The Times* for supplying two photographs used in one of my cottage articles, and with Alan from next door truly hooked Simon thought it would be worth a try. Sue had taken him to Mr Stevens' shop early in the holidays, brandishing a list of essentials prepared by a friend in London. The kitting out of a young fisherman is not a task to be taken at speed. Time went by, the official hour for lunchtime closing came and went, and eventually Simon emerged plus rod, reel, line and extras. I thought he would now be ready to rush off to 'The Cut' and catch his first pike, but I reckoned with out the practical element. Simon might have his tackle, but before it could be used, the line would have to be fed onto the reel, the question of how to weight the line, fix the float, learn to cast, and perhaps most important, how to bait the hook, all this had to be discussed, demonstrated and assimilated.

As I was saying: we had been buying maggots. Simon was raring to go and Sue was showing considerable enthusiasm too. It was early afternoon and we drove back to St Germans under a sky dulled only by a heat haze. Between Saddlebow and Fallow Pipe Road we first

137

saw the smoke, a black pall blackening the horizon apparently over our village. At first trees obscured our view: was it perhaps beyond St Germans, or on our side? Left turn at Fallow Pipe, past the house to which Don Noyce had recently moved, under the pylons and it became obvious that this was the field immediately down river from the Old Hall and, therefore, perhaps three hundred yards from Bank Cottage.

Did we panic? Not us. Although a ribbon of flame provided an erratic base to the smoke, we knew in a moment that someone was swaling – burning the stubble off the field. With the hot and dry summer, the harvest was three, four, even five weeks earlier than 1975, in itself unusually forward. We no longer screamed 'Fire!' every time we saw smoke across the Marshland landscape, but had advanced to remarking that no one seemed to be taking any notice of the widespread requests from government ministers and the National Farmers' Union to lay-off this year as the risks in fires spreading were too high thanks to the lack of rain. But properly controlled swaling should be safe; many farmers first plough round the perimeter of a field; others remove any surplus straw near boundaries or hedges.

Until now the swaling had all taken place at a distance, but here it was almost on our doorstep, and for the moment Simon's thoughts that had hitherto been devoted to making his debut with rod and line were now centred on the fire. We drove up Surrey Street, leapt out of the car, left the box of maggots on the wall by the front door and ran along the bank. We were not alone: John from the Crown and Anchor, Sally from next door, young Christopher, from the opposite bank – we all watched as the flames raced across the field towards us, fanned by the north-easterly wind. A team of men were on the field, encouraging the fire towards the odd patch of straw here, ensuring that nothing went amiss, when suddenly flames leapt off the stubble and into the tinder dry drainage ditch that separates the field from the river bank. With a new source of fuel the fire seemed to erupt along the ditch, consuming dying nettles, parched reeds and wild oats with which the ditch was infested. I should perhaps add

138

that I had an all too intimate acquaintance with this ditch. The previous week Simon and Edward, a boy from Highgate who was staying with us, had been flying a kite from the bank when a sudden down-draught grounded it in this very field, then ripe with uncut wheat. The boys pulled at the cord, but this became entangled and I was called in to attempt a rescue. The fence here is strands of barbed wire; immediately beyond is the ditch and then the wheat, which seemed very near. I clambered over the wire and leapt for the field, missed my footing and slipped back into the ditch, surrounded by nettles, fortunately dead as a result of the drought. Feeling foolish in front of two ten-year olds, I clawed myself back into view and stepped into the field. Should I plough straight across, regardless of the wheat? Or should I try to negotiate a path from the small islands of wheat flattened in some recent gale? In the end I chose the former, reckoning that any damage I might do would be slight, and nervous lest – in my ignorance – the field might be nurturing a nest of vipers. The kite was perhaps twenty yards into the field. I set out only to hear Simon shout: 'Sevenpence has gone in after you.' I looked around to see the tops of the wheat moving in an agitated way. Our labrador had no idea where he was as the height of the wheat blocked me from his view. I shouted, he heard, and eventually, after many false or perhaps more interesting scents he landed up by my legs and together we reached the kite, untangled it and headed back for the bank. This time I was determined not to repeat the misfortune of the outward journey, but I didn't have to puzzle a new way out. Sevenpence had obviously learnt from my ditchfall and had sniffed out a simpler alternative, by which he and I returned safely together.

All this was in the past. The fire continued to consume the contents of the ditch in the direction of the Old Hall. I could see Gerald, the Wallworks' gardener, watching anxiously. The farm men beat the itinerant flames with forks, someone discovered two ancient sheets of rusting corrugated iron which were brought into service as flame blankets. But more aid was needed. An ancient watering can – minus spout – was located. With a water trough for cattle twenty yards away, it suddenly took on new life. But Simon wasn't going to be left out. While Christopher rushed to help with the truncated watering can, Simon sped back to the cottage, grabbed a bucket from the garden and soon was part of a chain bringing water from the trough to where it was most needed – to quench the flames.

Meanwhile the rest of the field was black, with a few last embers producing wisps of smoke and the occasional final flames. And speedily, or so it seemed, the blaze in the ditch was brought under control, and minutes later extinguished. The observers turned for home, Christopher examined his singed boots, Simon was all smiles through a blackened face. All were agreed that it had been a near thing. If the blaze had remained unchecked it would have reached the Old Hall garden and once into that, first the Hall itself and then our cottages and the heart of St Germans might have been in danger. As it was only the Old Hall's trees bordering the field received a slight scorching.

The sweltering weather led to different theories about fishing. Some said that with water levels down the fish were nearer the surface and therefore easier to catch; others asserted that fish were far more sensible and stayed as deep as possible in order to remain cool. But whatever the truth Simon's fishing career this holiday got off to a frustrating beginning. While Alan Edwards and his cousin Paul were catching just about everything in sight, Simon had bites, but no catches. He was plagued with teething troubles, from a float that wouldn't float to a reel that kept getting tangled, but most surprisingly from inquisitive swans. 'Throw clods of earth at them' we were advised. We did and with much hissing and flapping they would desist.

I spent much of the time tinkering with the house. The hot weather had dried out the rendering almost too well with hairline cracks showing themselves on the river-facing frontage. I filled these and we discussed when we were going to do the painting. Sue suggested a postponement on the grounds that the three cottages next door were shortly going to be gutted and restored and we would feel most annoyed at freshly painted white rendering taking on a dusty hue in a matter of months. But I did borrow an extending ladder in order to secure the co-axial cable from the television aerial. Climbing almost to the top made me realize that my head for heights is not going to permit me to do the painting. We shall hire a professional hand to wield the brush.

My log for the period has weather as its theme. We did as bidden and put a brick in the cistern, but it interfered with the flushing mechanism and I made do with a bag full of pebbles. As I remarked in a previous chapter it was hardly the best year to establish a new garden, but by August we did begin to wonder if it would ever rain again. There were surprises, however: our courgettes were magnificent, producing a glut that helped fill our deep freeze: !ve tomato plants put in against the Old Hall boundary wall did magnificently, with the fruit that finally failed to ripen going for chutney. The maincrop potatoes kept on growing; the parsley better than I've ever seen before. I marvelled that we had no slugs, was saddened by the apparent lack of worms and cursed the cabbage white butterflies, whose caterpillers decimated the brassicas. On the bank bath- and dish-water helped keep many plants alive, but a number were lost. I soon realized from the weeding that anything with a tap root had the best chance of survival.

Life and work continued around us. Apart from the harvest we watched the now extravagantly-named Great Ouse River Division of the Anglian Water Authority in action on the bank near St Peters. It had been the old Great Ouse River Authority that had given us permission to tinker with the bank outside the cottage, now GORD (' . . . moves in mysterious ways' as someone was to remark in the pub) was reinforcing the bank. The work is known as 'pitching': layers of sand, different sizes of stone and willow mattresses combined with a final layer of stone being the best weapon against the scouring tides. It was a slow job; indeed friends told us that GORD had spent the best part of two years farther up river beyond Stow Bridge doing similar work.

My holiday was not without drama. The clutch cable of our Citroen snapped, but fortunately I was in second gear and managed to drive six miles to the nearest garage, without having to stop

141

despite a level crossing, two major road junctions and a set of traffic lights. A day or two later on a particularly high flood-tide I was just stepping into my bath when there was a shout from Sue upstairs. I donned jeans and rushed outside onto the bank to find Bob stretching over the bridge and holding an oar in order to stop his boat and the heavy wooden steps to which it was attached from floating away up river. I waded onto the flooded first level of the river bank and just managed to grab the boat painter.

In fact the high tides, although we did not know it at the time, signalled rain, and not just showers, but torrents. We were awoken on the Saturday before the August Bank Holiday by the sound of it lashing against the bedroom windows. Outside a large puddle formed on the path leading to our front door and water was pouring off the extension roof at such a rate that at one place it overshot the gutter (it didn't take long to move our new plastic dustbin to catch this niagara). The rain stopped, Simon and I walked up river to Magdalen and back and soon everywhere was steaming in the sun. We tested the garden and found that the rain had only wetted the surface. The following day it rained a little, but not spectacularly. We went blackberrying and discovered a bumper crop in the making. On Bank Holiday morning, under an overcast sky I dug a trench along the top of the bank in the hope that if it did rain the water would percolate into the bank, rather than run straight off.

As a matter of record it began to rain at St Germans at 1.30 p.m. just as we were sitting down to lunch. An hour later it was pouring steadily, within a further half an hour a puddle had formed again on our path. Friends arrived at this point and we had coffee. When at 3.45 p.m. we decided to show them our local churches it was raining buckets, so much so that our path was under water and our friends chose to leave the house by a downstairs window. I had left an old saucepan on the river-bank wall. We measured two inches of rain that afternoon, and the *Lynn News and Advertiser* a week later revealed that RAF Marham nearby recorded a record 4.138 inches between Saturday and Monday, with 2.41 inches on the Monday.

Here was the cue for nature's transformation scene. Within days

142

the grass was growing again, fields were green and our river bank sprouted the best crop of weeds I have ever seen.

Eight weeks later we were at Bank Cottage during the children's half-term. We dug four stones of potatoes from the back garden in a morning (and left a good quantity in situ), potatoes that at one period during the dry summer we had feared might turn out no larger than marbles. But the most astonishing sight for me came when I took Sevenpence for a walk down river, past the Old Hall and over the stile to the field where the stubble fire had got out of control. I looked at the ditch, expecting to see it still blackened from the flames. Not at all. Nature's transformation was complete. The wound had healed.